PROMOTING SMART TOURISM IN ASIA AND THE PACIFIC THROUGH DIGITAL COOPERATION

NOVEMBER 2023

ASIAN DEVELOPMENT BANK

CONTENTS

TABLES, FIGURES, AND BOXES

Boxes

ACKNOWLEDGMENTS

This publication was prepared by the Regional Cooperation and Integration Division (ERCI) of the Economic Research and Development Impact Department (ERDI), Asian Development Bank (ADB). Research for this publication was undertaken with financial support from ADB's regional knowledge and support technical assistance Strengthening Regional Cooperation and Integration Knowledge Partnerships and Research Network in Asia and the Pacific (TA 9537-REG). Publication and dissemination was supported under Strengthening Knowledge Alliance for Innovation, Technology, and Regional Cooperation (TA 9914-REG).

Jong Woo Kang, ERCI director, provided overall direction and supervision of the report.

Sanchita Basu-Das, economist, ERCI, led the study project from conceptualization to research and drafting of the report. Nishant Jain, director at Deloitte, and Josef Teofisto T. Yap, former president of the Philippine Institute for Development Studies, were part of the study team as ADB consultants to draft the report. Shubham Mahajan and Akshita Goyal from Deloitte and Mari Concepcion Latoja from ADB's Asia Regional Integration Center team provided research and data processing support.

The publication benefited from comments and suggestions provided by different departments of ADB.

Overall production was coordinated by Sanchita Basu-Das and Aleli Rosario, senior economics officer, ERCI. Marilyn Aure Parra facilitated discussions among team members throughout the period of study duration. Eric Van Zant edited the manuscript. Claudette Rodrigo created the cover design. Jonathan Yamongan did the layout and typesetting. Joy Quitazol-Gonzalez performed the proofreading, with support from Aleli Rosario and Carol Ongchangco. The Printing Services Unit of ADB's Corporate Services Department and the Publishing Team of the Department of Communications and Knowledge supported printing and publishing.

ABBREVIATIONS

ADB	Asian Development Bank
AI	artificial intelligence
APEC	Asia-Pacific Economic Cooperation
ASDEA	Australia–Singapore Digital Economy Agreement
ASEAN	Association of Southeast Asian Nations
CAREC	Central Asia Regional Economic Cooperation
COVID-19	coronavirus disease
CPTPP	Comprehensive and Progressive Agreement for Trans-Pacific Partnership
DEPA	Digital Economy Partnership Agreement
ICT	information and communication technology
IOT	Internet of Things
IP	intellectual property
MaaS	Mobility-as-a-Service
OECD	Organisation for Economic Co-operation and Development
PECC	Pacific Economic Cooperation Council
PPP	public–private partnership
RCEP	Regional Comprehensive Economic Partnership
SMEs	small and medium-sized enterprises
UNWTO	United Nations World Tourism Organization

EXECUTIVE SUMMARY

Tourism is a major sector in the global economy. International tourism receipts consistently rank among the top export categories in the world. The coronavirus disease (COVID-19) pandemic hit the tourism sector hard. In Asia and the Pacific, by the end of 2020, international tourist arrivals were down 84%, and over 50% of destinations were closed to international travel.

Efforts to recover from the pandemic and rebuild the tourism sector have focused on achieving sustainability, resilience, and inclusivity. "Build back better" or "build forward better" is gaining importance as it is about doing more than getting economies and livelihoods quickly back on track to pre-pandemic level. One way to restore and rebuild better is to pursue policies that encourage applications of digital technology for not only sustainable and inclusive outcome, but also to stimulate investment and behavioral changes that build resilience against shocks in the future.

This study explores ways to improve regional digital cooperation to expand the tourism industry—from traditional tourism to e-tourism to Tourism 4.0, and finally smart tourism. It classifies activities by tourism value chains and looks at digital technology through three lenses: Core information and communication technologies (ICTs), narrow scope (digital economy), and broad scope (digitalized economy). Convergence of digital technologies across applications can create dynamic innovation in a positive feedback loop between digitalization and the elements of the tourism value chain. Digitalization has varied across countries, however, leading to a digital divide, which is defined based on the stage of the digital journey relative to other countries. These stages can be classified as basic, intermediate, and advanced, and can relate to the degree of digitalization of the tourism sector.

Narrowing the digital divide and building smart tourism have been priorities for regional and international cooperation measures. Regional organizations, like the Association of Southeast Asian Nations (ASEAN), emphasize the importance of sustainability, environmental conservation, and sociocultural impacts in tourism planning. The Global Tourism Crisis Committee of the United Nations World Tourism Organization (UNWTO) identifies digital technology and supportive government policies as instruments in building more resilient and sustainable tourism. Both the Asian Development Bank (ADB) and the UNWTO recognize the potential that digitalization brings to the tourism sector in sustainable management and recovery.

Approach and Methodology of the Study

The study answers three key questions. First, to what extent can the tourism value chain be digitalized (module 1)? Second, given varied development of countries in a region, how ready are countries to implement smart tourism practices (module 2)? Third, how can regional digital cooperation be improved to promote smart tourism in a region (module 3)?

The study's systematic approach uses three modules to answer the three questions. It includes a secondary review of the tourism value chain and its activities, as well as the digital technologies that can drive transformation in the tourism economy. By mapping the applications of digital technologies to different elements of value chain activities, the capacity of smart tourism to build back better is evaluated. Using the four principles of smart tourism (attractiveness, accessibility, sustainability, and collaborative partnership), smart tools are described for the two components of smart tourism: smart destination and smart travel. Meanwhile, country case studies are utilized to gain insights into specific practices in this context.

To maintain the competitive edge in global tourism, nations have adopted the four principles of smart tourism to varying levels. In this study, selected ASEAN member countries are used as samples to understand the similarities and differences across countries in adopting smart tourism practices.

Finally, the study compares four digital agreements—The Australia–Singapore Digital Economy Agreement, the Digital Economy Partnership Agreement, the Comprehensive and Progressive Agreement for Trans-Pacific Partnership, and the Regional Comprehensive Economic Partnership—based on how they address digital economy and trade in services issues. The agreements highlight key areas across issues that can be resolved through sharing of best practices, creating strategic frameworks, and finding common grounds in legal structures in the digital economy. The study concludes with policy recommendations across digital economy cooperation issues with implications for tourism in a region. The figure below shows the framework for the entire study.

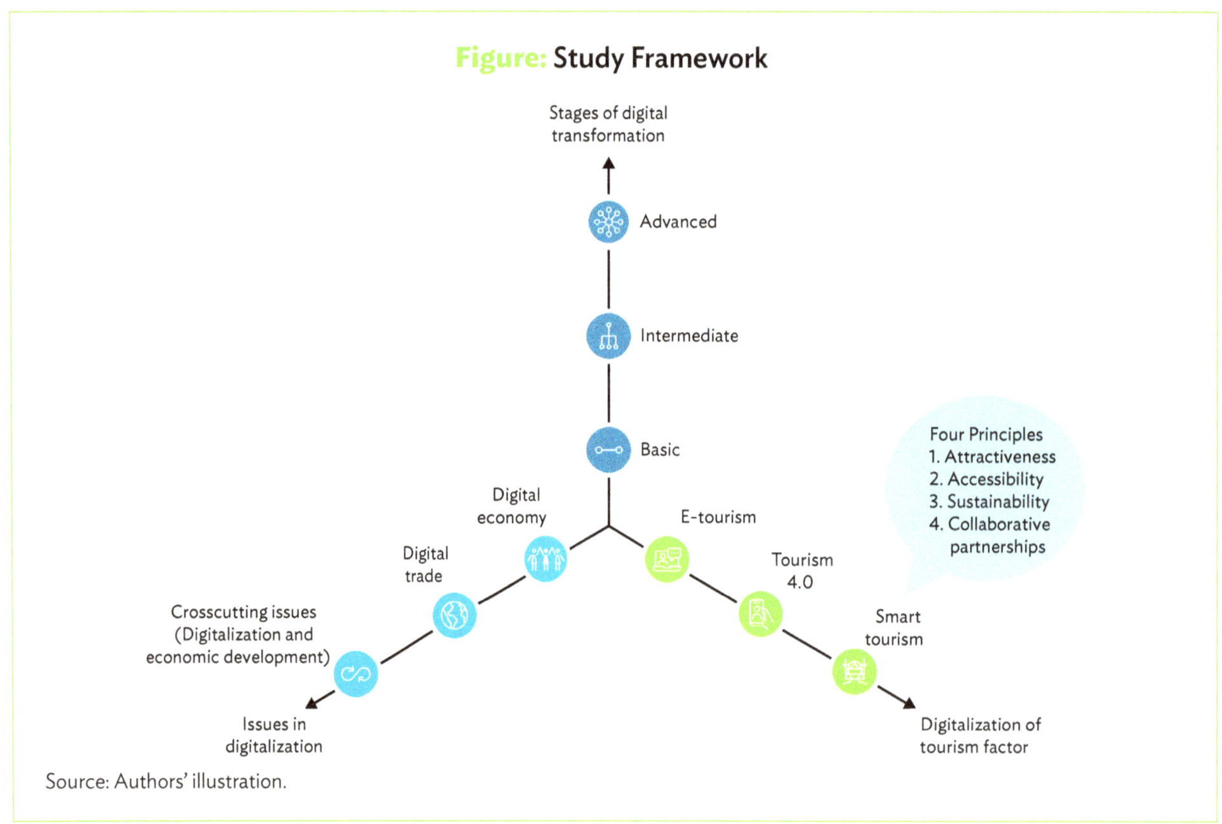

Source: Authors' illustration.

Module 1: Tourism Value Chain and Digital Transformation

Smart tourism is the evolved form of traditional and e-tourism, in which the data collected from physical infrastructure and tourism stakeholders are transformed into actionable insights and viable business propositions using advanced technologies. Smart tourism has two major components: smart travel and smart destination. Smart travel covers use of advanced technology in services and activities related to getting the tourist from origin to destination. Meanwhile, smart destination facilitates access to tourism services, spaces, and experiences through ICT-based tools to maximize a tourist's satisfaction.

As the digital revolution transformed traditional tourism to e-tourism and, later, to smart tourism, the latter was conceptualized through four key principles.

- "Attractiveness" refers to the degree to which tangible and intangible experiences are provided using advanced technologies from the Fourth Industrial Revolution.
- "Accessibility" refers to how accessible tourist information and transportation are virtually and physically and how advanced technologies and design principles have been tapped to create inclusive tourism experiences for people with disabilities, seniors, and others with specific needs.
- "Sustainability" is crucial in determining the foundation for social, economic, and environmental growth in smart tourism cities or places, encompassing factors like resilience, safety, creativity, innovation, renewable energy use, responsible tourism practices, cultural exchange, job creation, and economic competitiveness.
- "Collaborative partnership" refers to partnership between the different stakeholders of a smart tourism ecosystem.

Using case studies from around the world, it is determined that the entire tourism value chain—consisting of smart travel and smart destination—can be digitally transformed. For example, under smart travel, technological advances in biometrics have produced digital solutions that enable identity verification for a frictionless journey; better security, health, and safety; and commercial benefits. Likewise, smart destinations that use ICT-based tools and integrated platforms can ease access to tourism and hospitality products and services to enhance tourist satisfaction.

Module 2: Assessment of Readiness of Selected ASEAN Member Countries for Smart Tourism

The ASEAN region has recognized the importance of sustainable tourism and digital transformation, as evidenced by its tourism strategy and the Declaration on Digital Tourism. The goal has been to promote newer, value-adding economic activities, preserve the natural environment, and provide high-quality experiences to responsible tourists. Due to various critical factors of policy, society, and demography, the member countries are at different stages of realizing the potential of digitalization and, hence, accelerating growth of the tourism sector. The study uses secondary data from various sources to assess progress in selected ASEAN members toward smart tourism. It quantifies readiness across the four principles just discussed. The analysis focuses on the adoption of digital products and services in the tourism sector, examining disparities within countries and between countries in the same region.

The analytical exercise benchmarks Singapore as the group leader for its readiness in smart tourism, reinforcing its highest rank on digitalization. Attributes include smart governance, accessibility, smart mobility, sustainability, and barrier-free design. Malaysia and Thailand follow Singapore for most of the attributes, though wide disparity remains in their digital readiness. The analysis in this module shows that the digital divide, while a hindrance for making ASEAN a single smart tourist destination, also provides opportunities for bilateral and regional cooperation.

Module 3: Comparison of Regional Cooperation Mechanisms for Deeper Digital Economy

In order to advance digitalization in the tourism sector and the economy as a whole, policymakers need to address the regulatory gaps at national and regional levels. This is in addition to ICT infrastructure connectivity. Using the digital economy framework proposed by the Pacific Economic Cooperation Council, this part of the report looks at the four digital agreements that some of the region's economies have joined recently to understand how these may facilitate smart tourism in the region, as summarized in Table A. The Australia–Singapore Digital Economy Agreement and the Digital Economy Partnership Agreement are more comprehensive for strengthening digital cooperation than the Comprehensive and Progressive Agreement for Trans-Pacific Partnership and the Regional Comprehensive Economic Partnership, where the agenda of cooperation goes beyond the digital economy. This implies that countries in the first two agreements are more likely to adopt smart tourism practices with greater spillover effects on the rest of the economy.

Table A: **Comparing Features of Regional Mechanisms that Address Digital Cooperation**

Issue	Relevant Chapters	ASDEA		DEPA		CPTPP		RCEP	
Digital Economy									
Data protection and privacy	Personal information protection	✓	+	✓	+	✓	–	✓	–
	Cryptography	✓		✓		✗		✗	
Cybersecurity	Cybersecurity	✓	+	✓	+	✓	–	✓	–
Competition policy	Nondiscrimination of digital products	✓		✓		✓		✗	
	Cooperation on competition policy[a]	✓	+	✓	+	✓	–	✓	–
Intellectual property	Source code	✓	+	✗		✓	–	✗	
	Intellectual property	✗		✓	–	✓	+	✓	+
Consumer protection	Online consumer protection	✓	+	✓	+	✓	–	✓	–
	Spam (Unsolicited messages)	✓		✓		✓		✓	
	Safe online environment	✓	+	✓	–	✗		✗	
Digital identity	Digital identity	✓		✓		✗		✗	
	Electronic signature/authentication	✓		✗		✓		✓	
Data sharing	Open government data	✓		✓		✗		✗	
Quality of service	Standards and conformity assessment	✓		✗		✗		✗	
	Dispute settlement[a]	✓		✓		✓		✓	
Artificial intelligence	AI or emerging technologies	✓		✓		✗		✗	

continued on next page

Table on Features of Regional Mechanisms continued

Issue	Relevant Chapters	ASDEA	DEPA	CPTPP	RCEP
Digital Trade					
Cross-border data flows	Allowing data flow	✓ +	✓ +	✓ +	✓ −
	Data localization	✓	✓	✓	✓
	Data localization for financial services	✓	✗	✗	✗
	Custom duties	✓ −	✓ −	✓ −	✓ +
Data transfer mechanisms	Domestic e-transaction framework	✓ +	✓ +	✓ −	✓ −
Digital trade standards	E-invoicing	✓	✓	✗	✗
	E-payments	✓	✓	✗	✗
Regulatory fragmentation and regulatory arbitrage	Transparency[a]	✓ −	✓ +	✓ +	✓ −
	Express shipments[a]	✓	✓	✓	✓
	Fintech and regulatory tech cooperation	✓ +	✓ −	✗	✗
Crosscutting Issues					
Inclusivity and digital divide	Access to and use of internet[a]	✓ −	✓ −	✓ +	✓ +
	Digital inclusion	✗	✓	✗	✗
	Interconnection charges[a]	✓ −	✗	✓ +	✓ +
	Stakeholder engagement	✓ +	✗	✗	✓ −
Digital development	Data innovation	✓	✓	✗	✗
	Submarine cable[a]	✓ +	✗	✓ −	✓ −
Digitalization of big and small enterprises	SMEs[a]	✓ +	✓ +	✓ −	✓ −
Green digitalization	Paperless trading	✓ +	✓ +	✓ −	✓ −

✗ No provision   ✓ Identical or nearly identical provisions   ✓ − Less comprehensive provision   ✓ + More comprehensive provision

AI = artificial intelligence, ASDEA = Australia–Singapore Digital Economy Agreement, CPTPP = Comprehensive and Progressive Agreement for Trans-Pacific Partnership, DEPA = Digital Economy Partnership Agreement, RCEP = Regional Comprehensive Economic Partnership, SMEs = small and medium-sized enterprises.

[a] The CPTPP and the RCEP cover these topics in a chapter separate from the chapter on e-commerce.

Source: Authors' compilation based on agreement texts.

Policy Recommendations to Pave the Way Forward

Digitalization has emerged as a crucial tool to aid the tourism sector's recovery and promote long-term resilience, inclusivity, and sustainability. The objectives of build back better are being attained, as advanced technologies in the Fourth Industrial Revolution are integrated into most components of the tourism sector and the economy in general. This study recommends policies for regional groupings to develop a framework that helps national governments strengthen regional cooperation for digital transformation and, hence, accelerate the growth of the tourism sector. This will provide opportunities to tourism stakeholders to improve efficiency, enhance customer experiences, personalize offerings, and adapt to the evolving needs and expectations of modern travelers. This will have further benefits for the wider economy in general. Table B identifies themes relevant for the development of smart tourism (such as data protection and privacy), recognizes issues related to them (such as cryptography), and lists actionable policies for greater cooperation.

Table B: Policy Recommendations to Strengthen Digital Economy Cooperation for Smart Tourism

Issue		Recommendations
1. Data Protection and Privacy		
The tourism industry generates huge amounts of data that could be personal and sensitive in nature and, hence, be a potential target for cybercriminals. This makes it important that the data is well protected and provided to authorized parties only on user's consent.		
1.1	Cryptography	• Strengthening encryption standards through multistakeholder collaboration and legislative protection • Promoting encryption education and awareness • Harmonizing relevant policies and standards that impact encryption • Balancing security and privacy • Protecting information and communications technology products using cryptography
2. Intellectual Property		
Intellectual property (IP) systems provide a regulatory framework aiming to foster innovation and creativity. IP rights in tourism have various benefits such as enhancing management of companies and tourism destinations, differentiating tourism destinations and products from competitors, attracting investment and financing especially for small and medium-sized enterprises, etc.[a]		
2.1	Source Code	• Strengthening IP protection through legislative actions • Creating mechanisms to ensure strict enforcement of nondisclosure agreements • Encouraging secure code collaboration platforms
3. Consumer Protection		
In digital economy, where most of the interactions between consumers and businesses happen online, digital consumers face challenges such as misleading ratings or reviews, scams, fraud, etc.[b] These issues can make consumers lose trust in online marketplaces and e-commerce, especially for cross-border transactions because of regulatory differences. Tourism industry is most vulnerable to frauds, with digital frauds in travel and leisure industry rising (111% during 2019–2021).[c]		
3.1	Safe Online Environment	• Creating incident response and reporting mechanisms • Encouraging multistakeholder collaboration
4. Digital Identity		
From a tourist's point of view, digital identities make travel seamless, secure, and safe, while governments and businesses can benefit from secure screening and identification (ID) of travellers. Many countries have already implemented one form of digital ID or ePassport; however, there is still scope for collaboration between countries to benefit from making interoperable systems across multiple sectors.		
4.1	Digital Identity	• Promoting interoperability and compatibility of digital ID systems • Promoting inclusion and accessibility
5. Data Sharing		
Data is an important resource for economic growth, competitiveness, job creation, and societal progress.[d] Maintaining open datasets can benefit multiple stakeholders. Various regions like Europe have already implemented open data portals, which provide datasets on various sectors including tourism.[e]		
5.1	Open Government Data	• Developing open-data policies • Maintaining accessible data portals

continued on next page

Table on Policy Recommendations continued

Issue		Recommendations
6. Quality of Service		
Ensuring delivery of quality service is important for maintaining higher levels of customer satisfaction. The same fundamental holds true for the tourism economy.		
6.1	Standards and Conformity Assessment	• Promoting adoption of international standards • Harmonizing of regulatory requirements
7. Artificial Intelligence		
Artificial intelligence (AI) presents huge opportunities for tourists, businesses, and governments with applications like chatbots, predictive analysis, automation, etc. Despite these benefits, AI still faces regulatory challenges because of the unpredictable nature of business models relying on these technologies, data privacy, security, ownership, and control issues, and the complex nature as opposed to traditional software.[f]		
7.1	AI and Emerging Technologies	• Developing ethical and responsible regulatory frameworks for AI governance
8. Cross-Border Data Flows		
Cross-border data flows are essential to economic growth in the digital economy. For tourism, this means free flow of data across borders for businesses and governments.		
8.1	Data Localization for Financial Services	• Following risk-based approaches to data localization requirement • Providing regulatory clarity and certainty • Promoting flexibility on requirement of location of computing facilities for financial services
9. Digital Trade Standards		
Digital trade standards ensure interoperability among different digital platforms and enable smooth integration of diverse services for an enhanced tourist experience. The standardization also secures data transmission, thereby building trust in digital transactions and encouraging more tourists to adopt the smart tourism services.		
9.1	E-invoicing	• Promoting standardization and interoperability • Strengthening integration with business systems • Mandating or incentivizing adoption
9.2	E-payments	• Investing in digital payment infrastructure • Promoting interoperability and standardization • Providing regulatory framework for information sharing
10. Regulatory Fragmentation:		
The lack of harmonization between regulations and laws leads to slower adoption of smart tourism practices and technologies as businesses will hesitate to invest in sectors and regions having complex and conflicting regulations. The inconsistency in legal frameworks results in higher compliance costs and administrative burdens, thereby impeding innovation and hindering collaboration between regions.		
10.1	Fintech and Regulatory Tech Cooperation	• Promoting regulatory sandboxes for cross-border testing • Strengthening regulatory agility • Adopting proportional regulation

continued on next page

Table on Policy Recommendations continued

Issue		Recommendations
11. Inclusivity and Digital Divide		
Bridging the digital divide establishes a sustainable tourism environment. Strategies like expanding connectivity, providing digital skills training, fostering digital innovation, and designing user-friendly interfaces can address the digital divide among tourists.		
11.1	Digital Inclusion	• Supporting infrastructure development • Providing local content and multilingual support • Establishing digital inclusion metrics and monitoring
11.2	Stakeholder Engagement	• Organizing multistakeholder platforms • Encouraging participation of grassroots organizations and communities • Supporting early capacity building
12. Digital Development and Use of Big Data		
Digital development may include development of data governance framework, open data initiatives, ethical and responsible data use, and data impact assessment. Policy recommendations related to these issues have been discussed under various headings above.		

[a] World Intellectual Property Organization (WIPO) and United Nations World Tourism Organization. 2021. *Boosting Tourism Development through Intellectual Property*. Geneva: WIPO.

[b] Organisation for Economic Co-operation and Development. 2021. *The Role of Online Marketplaces in Enhancing Consumer Protection*. Paris.

[c] TransUnion. 2022. *Global Digital Fraud Trends: Rising Customer Expectations amid Evolving Fraud Threats*. https://www.transunion.com/content/dam/transunion/global/business/documents/2022-fraud-trends-report.pdf.

[d] European Commission. A European Strategy for Data. https://digital-strategy.ec.europa.eu/en/policies/strategy-data.

[e] Europaen Commission. Eurostat. EU Tourism Database. https://ec.europa.eu/eurostat/web/tourism/data/database (accessed July 2023).

[f] Digital Regulation Platform. 2020. Elements of Spectrum Management for Upcoming Technologies. 9 February. https://digitalregulation.org/3004297-2/e.

Source: Asian Development Bank.

1 Tourism and Digitalization: Keys to the Post-Pandemic Recovery

The coronavirus disease (COVID-19) pandemic revealed the vulnerability of the tourism sector, but it also provided an opportunity to address sector weaknesses. Digitalization is increasingly being considered as a way to strengthen economic recovery and make it more resilient, inclusive, and sustainable. The challenge is to create a smart tourism ecosystem where digitalization and tourism can come together. Regional cooperation can build synergies between tourism and digitalization, but the digital divide between and within countries in a region has to be narrowed for it to be more effective—in this, too, regional cooperation can help.

This report details policy recommendations at the regional level to enhance the smart tourism ecosystem and narrow the digital divide. This chapter, particularly, presents the objectives, framework, and methodology of the study and discusses its underlying concepts, including the tourism value chain, the process of digitalization, and the two pillars of smart tourism ecosystem. Regional cooperation for a smart tourism ecosystem is the center of the study's policy recommendations.

Build Back Better

Tourism's Contribution to the Global Economy

Tourism is one of the major sectors in the global economy. It was the world's third largest export category after fuels and chemicals, and ahead of automotive products and food in the 2019 accounting for 7% of global exports.[1] Data from the United Nations World Tourism Organization (UNWTO) show that, globally, international tourist receipts during the last 2 decades peaked before COVID-19 in 2020 (Figure 1), with similar trends in Asia and the Pacific.

Indeed, tourism was among the hardest-hit sectors, as the pandemic lockdowns impacted incomes, livelihoods, public services, and economic opportunities. Tourist arrivals globally—the flipside of revenues—peaked in 2019 (Figure 2) and fell by 72% in 2020, with Asia and the Pacific recording the largest regional decline (Figure 3). Worse still, the region's global share of tourist arrivals also shrank. Abbas et al. (2021) estimates that global leisure, travel, and inbound tourism lost a combined $2.86 trillion in 2020, equivalent to about a 50% loss in revenues.

---

[1]   United Nations World Tourism Organization (UNWTO). 2021. International Tourism Highlights. 2020 Edition. Madrid. https://doi.org/10.18111/9789284422456.

Figure 1: **International Tourism Receipts, Asia and the Pacific versus World, 2010–2022**
($ billion)

Sources: Asia and the Pacific values from United Nations World Tourism Organization (UNWTO). 2022. Compendium of Tourism Statistics dataset [Electronic] (accessed November 2022); and World values from UNWTO. UNWTO Tourism Data Dashboard. https://www.unwto.org/tourism-data/unwto-tourism-dashboard (accessed 10 November 2022).

Figure 2: **International Tourist Arrivals, Asia and the Pacific versus World, 2010–2022**
(millions)

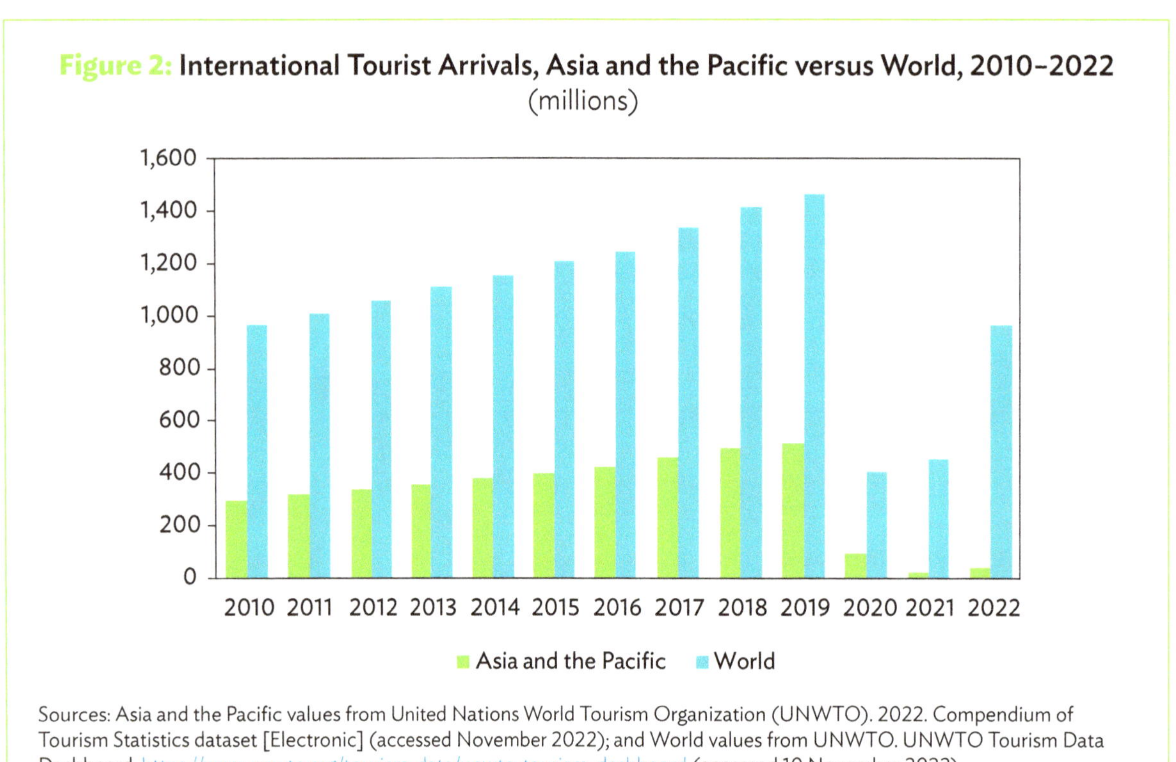

Sources: Asia and the Pacific values from United Nations World Tourism Organization (UNWTO). 2022. Compendium of Tourism Statistics dataset [Electronic] (accessed November 2022); and World values from UNWTO. UNWTO Tourism Data Dashboard. https://www.unwto.org/tourism-data/unwto-tourism-dashboard (accessed 10 November 2022).

Source: United Nations World Tourism Organization. UNWTO Tourism Data Dashboard. https://www.unwto.org/tourism-data/unwto-tourism-dashboard (accessed 25 July 2023).

Nonetheless, clear signs of recovery emerged in 2022 as countries resumed allowing visitors. Figure 2 and Figure 3 show a slight recovery in the tourism sector in 2021, accelerating in 2022. However, stricter and longer border and quarantine restriction measures compared to other regions slowed the pace in Asia and the Pacific.

Building Back Better through Digitalization and Regional Cooperation

Stronger recovery is needed for a resilient, inclusive, and sustainable outcome, in keeping with the mantras of "build back better" or "build forward better," which are guiding efforts to overcome the pandemic. The Organisation for Economic Co-operation and Development (OECD) has declared that economic recovery from the pandemic should extend beyond rapidly restoring jobs and businesses. Policies that support revitalization need to encourage activities that will reduce the likelihood of future disruptions and enhance society's resilience to them when they do occur (OECD 2022a).

Regional organizations, such as the Association of Southeast Asian Nations (ASEAN), have likewise agreed that recovery from the pandemic should involve setting up a more sustainable tourism sector that promotes resilience (ERIA 2022). In particular, sustainability must be pivotal in all subsequent tourism planning in the region. Adequate consideration should also be given to climate change and environmental issues and to crucial sociocultural impacts of tourism.

In these efforts, digital technology and supportive government policies encouraging public and private sectors to adopt smart tourism have been gaining importance. As countries lifted the travel restrictions, UNWTO convened the Global Tourism Crisis Committee to monitor and guide the sector as it responded to the pandemic and to lay the groundwork for future resilience and sustainability. It identified seven priorities (Figure 4): the first five are mitigative, and the last two priorities deal with building resilience in the sector, predominantly through digitalization (UNWTO 2020).

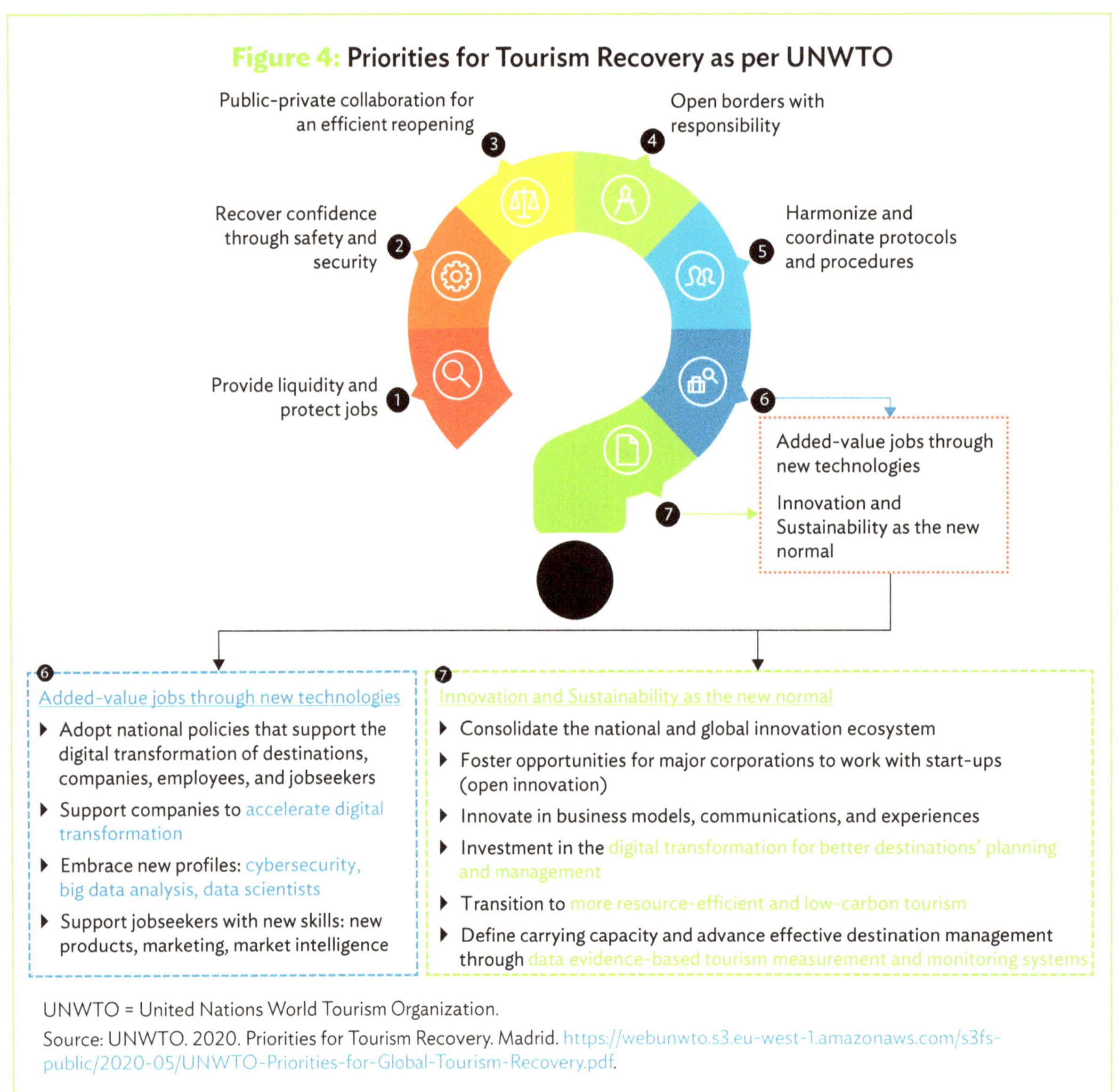

Figure 4: Priorities for Tourism Recovery as per UNWTO

UNWTO = United Nations World Tourism Organization.
Source: UNWTO. 2020. Priorities for Tourism Recovery. Madrid. https://webunwto.s3.eu-west-1.amazonaws.com/s3fs-public/2020-05/UNWTO-Priorities-for-Global-Tourism-Recovery.pdf.

A recent report by the Asian Development Bank (ADB) and UNWTO (2021) discusses how big data and digitalization can benefit the sector and help achieve more sustainable tourism management and recovery. Tourism-specific data emanating from sources such as tourism operators and online platforms—and nontourism-specific data from sources such as credit card transactions, mobility services, and sensors—can enable tourism stakeholders to track and manage the social, economic, and environmental impacts of tourism activities. Such data can complement more traditional data, control tourism flows, and prioritize preferred source markets, helping to promote smart destinations.

Meanwhile, the role of regional cooperation in Asia and the Pacific is considered, since tourism value chains span international borders. The elements of those value chains, therefore, operate under different national ecosystems, which are influenced by local capabilities. Moreover, some countries can benefit from the experience and successful practices of their neighbors. Hence, the success of digitalization in tourism requires collaboration and cooperation of nations in initiatives spanning knowledge sharing, joint marketing, infrastructure development, skill building, and policy coordination.

About the Study

Objectives

This study analyzes and discusses smart tourism in detail and assesses country readiness and the role of regional cooperation. It examines the tourism value chain and components of digitalization that underpin the smart tourism ecosystem. It empirically assesses selected countries from the region at different levels of development for their readiness in adopting smart tourism practices. It also examines the principles of digital trade agreements to identify gaps in leading regional digital cooperation initiatives that may enable countries to adopt smart tourism practices, promoting international tourism in a region. It recommends policy choices in how regional cooperation could be strengthened to deliver smart tourism objectives, as articulated in national and regional policy documents.

The study's five chapters answer three research questions:

- To what extent can the activities in the tourism value chain undergo digital transformation?
- How far are countries ready to adopt digital transformation in their tourism sector, particularly given their varied development levels?
- How is digital economy cooperation featured in the latest regional cooperation mechanisms, given that countries participating in digital economy agreements may have greater potential to adopt smart tourism practices?

Study Framework

Figure 5 shows the basic framework tying together the research questions. A more elaborate framework, underpinned by the four principles of smart tourism—attractiveness, accessibility, sustainability, and collaborative partnership—is discussed in Chapter 2. The study analyzes three strands: (i) the degree of digitalization of the tourism sector—from e-tourism to Tourism 4.0 to smart tourism; (ii) the stage of a country's digital transformation, which can be basic, intermediate, or advanced; and (iii) the core issues that have to be addressed to advance digitalization of the tourism sector and the economy as a whole. Regional cooperation is a means by which these core issues can be addressed.

Subsequent chapters will explain the various concepts and how the three strands interact. The different threads, tied together, essentially form the smart tourism ecosystem.

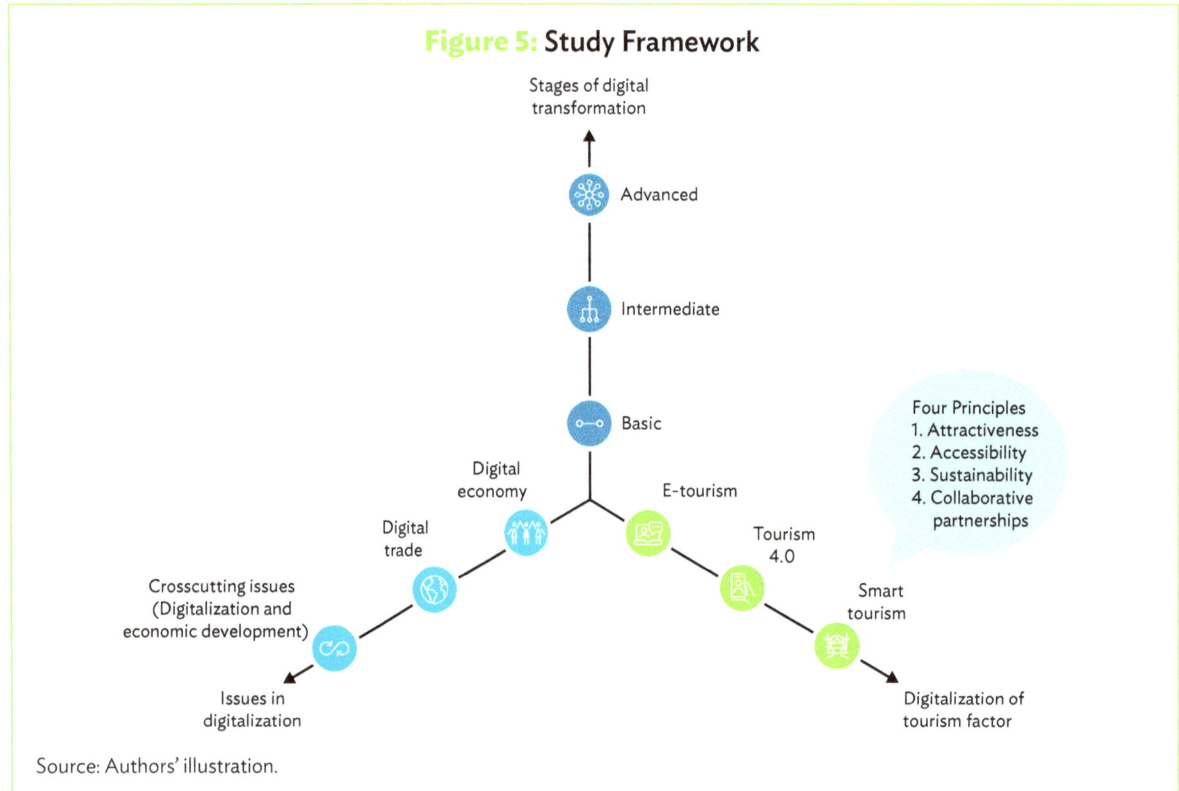

Figure 5: Study Framework

Source: Authors' illustration.

Methodology

The methodology is based on a three-module approach, in line with the research questions and the framework.

Module 1—Unpacking Smart Tourism

This is Chapter 2 of the report, which expands on the first strand of the framework—the degree of digitalization in the tourism sector. In this module, tourism value chain activities are identified, along with different digital technologies capable of transforming the tourism economy. The amenability of the digital technologies is then gauged to the different tourism value chain activities. Evaluation of the tourism value chain's propensity to adopt technology will help define the interface between the stage of a country's digital transformation and the degree of digitalization of the tourism industry. Country case studies are used to understand specific practices.

Module 2—Country Readiness to Adopt Smart Tourism Practices

Chapter 3 of the report builds on the second strand of the framework—the stage of an economy's digital transformation. The module uses secondary data from various sources to examine country readiness to adopt smart tourism practices. It looks at selected Southeast Asian countries to analyze the digital divide both within and between countries of the same region. This allows consideration of the opportunities and constraints to regional cooperation, which is tackled in the next module.

Module 3—Gaps in Regional Digital Economy Cooperation Agreements

This module (Chapter 4) focuses on the regional component of the core issues. It looks at supply side enablers for building smart tourism across countries. The discussion lays down the provisions of the digital economy, digital trade, and crosscutting issues, and identifies gaps in discussing the same in the regional cooperation documents of Australia–Singapore Digital Economy Agreement (ASDEA), Digital Economy Partnership Agreement (DEPA), Comprehensive and Progressive Agreement for Trans-Pacific Partnership (CPTPP), and Regional Comprehensive Economic Partnership (RCEP).

Key Concepts of the Study

The Tourism Value Chain and the Complex System

The tourism sector's value chain comprises of various segments with different actors. The destination is the most important foundation for tourism services (GIZ 2020). This includes the natural and sociocultural resources and the basic infrastructure, such as access roads and energy supply. Figure 6 presents the traditional view of the value chain for the tourism sector, i.e., a sequence of value-adding activities involved in the production and delivery of product or service.

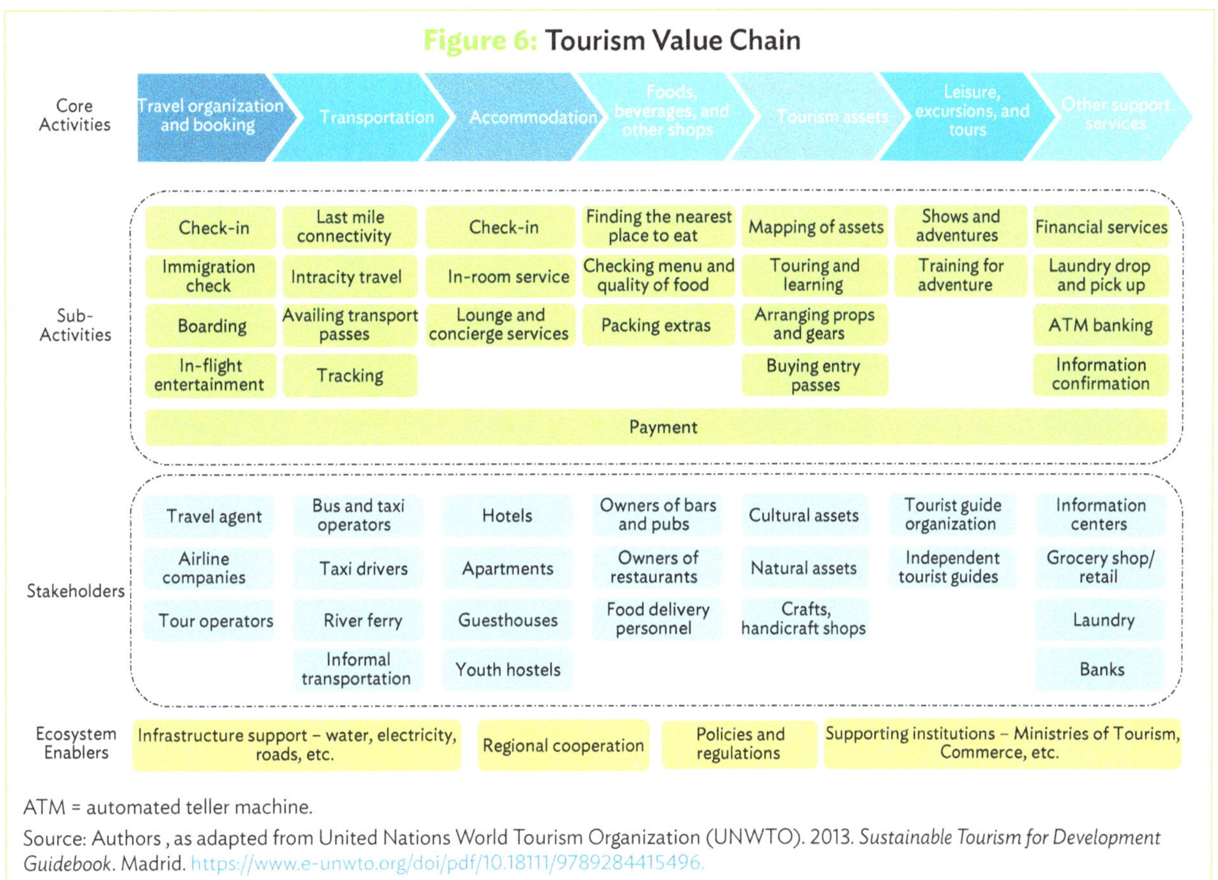

Figure 6: Tourism Value Chain

Sub-Activities						
Check-in	Last mile connectivity	Check-in	Finding the nearest place to eat	Mapping of assets	Shows and adventures	Financial services
Immigration check	Intracity travel	In-room service	Checking menu and quality of food	Touring and learning	Training for adventure	Laundry drop and pick up
Boarding	Availing transport passes	Lounge and concierge services	Packing extras	Arranging props and gears		ATM banking
In-flight entertainment	Tracking			Buying entry passes		Information confirmation
Payment						

Stakeholders						
Travel agent	Bus and taxi operators	Hotels	Owners of bars and pubs	Cultural assets	Tourist guide organization	Information centers
Airline companies	Taxi drivers	Apartments	Owners of restaurants	Natural assets	Independent tourist guides	Grocery shop/ retail
Tour operators	River ferry	Guesthouses	Food delivery personnel	Crafts, handicraft shops		Laundry
	Informal transportation	Youth hostels				Banks

Ecosystem Enablers			
Infrastructure support – water, electricity, roads, etc.	Regional cooperation	Policies and regulations	Supporting institutions – Ministries of Tourism, Commerce, etc.

ATM = automated teller machine.

Source: Authors , as adapted from United Nations World Tourism Organization (UNWTO). 2013. *Sustainable Tourism for Development Guidebook*. Madrid. https://www.e-unwto.org/doi/pdf/10.18111/9789284415496.

Tourism destinations, often a part of complexity theory, encompass numerous interdependent factors and activities with relationships that might be highly nonlinear (Baggio 2008). Figure 7 illustrates these relationships through a casual loop diagram. The basic tenets of complexity theory are non-linear dynamics, and adaptation or evolution; others include emergence, self-organization, feedback, and chaos (Turner and Baker 2019). The symptoms of complexity, which also appear in the tourism sector, are as follows (Baggio 2008):

- a large number of elements form the system;
- interactions among the elements are nonlinear;
- there are loops in the interactions;
- complex systems are usually open and their state is far from equilibrium;
- complex systems have a history, the "future" behavior depends on the past one; and
- each element is unaware of the behavior of the system as a whole, it reacts only to information available to it locally.

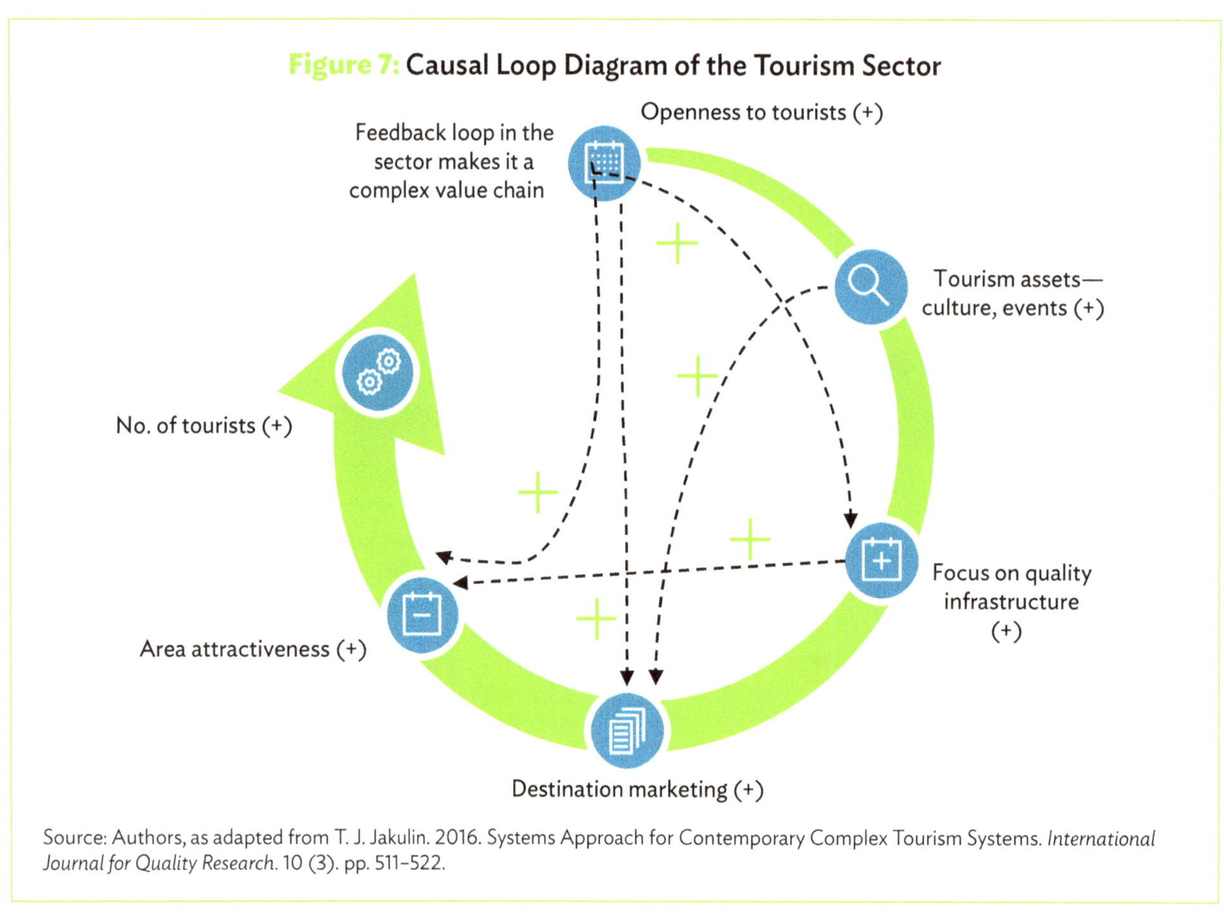

Figure 7: Causal Loop Diagram of the Tourism Sector

Source: Authors, as adapted from T. J. Jakulin. 2016. Systems Approach for Contemporary Complex Tourism Systems. *International Journal for Quality Research*. 10 (3). pp. 511–522.

Generation of positive feedback loops or cycles can be highlighted as the basis to evaluate proposed policies related to digitalization. The interactions among the components of the system become more critical than their own individual features and the resulting feedback cycles can impact the overall behavior of the system. The relevance of tourism as a complex system comes into focus when the smart tourism ecosystem is detailed in Chapter 2.

Digitalization and Tourism

Digitalization of economic activities started with the evolution and growing use of information and communication technology (ICT). It is often viewed as the "incorporation of data and the Internet into production processes and products, new forms of household and government consumption, fixed-capital formation, cross-border flows, and finance" (IMF 2018). Digitalization is transforming the services sector, with wide-ranging applications in retail markets, the financial sector, and many others.

Tourism is increasingly seen as a sector where digitalization has the potential to boost innovation, generate economic and environmental efficiencies, and increase productivity (OECD 2020b). Table 1 shows how elements of tourism value chain are amenable to digitalization. This is an example of how tourists' experience is enhanced by the application of digital interventions.

Table 1: **User Journey of a Tourist Travelling to Europe**

Tourism Value Chain	Technology-Driven Experiences
Travel Organization and Booking	• Destination government website, **Visit Europe**, helps to disseminate information about the destination. • Tourism agent websites like **TripAdvisor** and **MakeMyTrip** allow travelers to get additional information. • **Artificial intelligence (AI)-driven chatbots** help to solve travellers' queries efficiently. • Blogs by travel influencers, such as **Salt in our hair**, allow travellers to understand the on-ground reality. • Social media helps to spread the information in effective and faster ways.
Aviation and Transport	• Online Travel Agents, like **Booking.com**, allows travelers to compare prices and book tickets online. • Europe's **Schengen Visa** makes the visa application process completely online and hassle-free. • Shared economy apps, like **Taxi EU**, allow travellers to get a taxi within minutes. • Super apps, like **Omio**, helps travellers book tickets for trains, rails, buses, ferries, etc. through a single platform. • Traffic management systems, such **Snap4City**, helps cities like Florence, Italy to manage the traffic.
Accommodation	• Companies, like **Airbnb**, provide online accommodation marketplaces making it easier to find accommodation anywhere in the country. • In-hotel mobile apps, like **Virgin Hotel's Lucy**, provide a wide range of services, from ordering the food to acting as a room key and even for controlling room lights.
Food, Beverage, and Shopping	• Mobile applications, like **Grubhub**, let travelers reserve the seats at their favorite restaurant. • Ghost kitchens, like **Keatz**, provide food delivery service right at the doorstep. • Platforms, such as **Tock To Go**, allows tourists to pre-order their meal for a future time and date.
Tourism Assets, Leisure, and Tours	• Mobile applications, like **Terra Aventura** app, provide a family treasure hunt game experience in France with 400 unusual discroutes to over the natural and cultural heritage. • Self-guide apps, such as **Nexto** app, are innovative smart audio city guide in Slovenia, which engages its users through features like puzzles, riddles, and item collection by mobile scanning and augmented reality (AR). • **Virtual bicycling experience** in Copenhagen gives travelers a taste of cycling in the city without actually riding one.

Sources: Airbnb. https://www.airbnb.com/, Booking.com https://www.booking.com/, Cycling Embassy of Denmark.https://cyclingsolutions.info/embassy/virtual-reality-bike-tour-copenhagen/, EU Startups – Keatz. https://www.eu-startups.com/directory/keatz/, Grubhub. https://www.grubhub.com/, MakeMyyTrip. https://www.makemytrip.com/, Nexto. https://nexto.io/, Omio. https://www.omio.com/, Salt in Our Hair. https://www.saltinourhair.com/, SchengenVisa. https://www.schengenvisainfo.com/, Snao4city – Firenze Smart City Control Room. https://www.snap4city.org/drupal/node/531, Taxi EU. https://www.taxi.eu/en/, Terra Adventure. https://www.terra-aventura.fr/en/how-play, Tock To Go. https://www.exploretock.com/togo/, Tripadvisor. https://www.tripadvisor.com/, Virgin Hotels. https://virginhotels.com/about-the-app/, and Visit Europe. https://visiteurope.com/en/destinations/.

These technology applications in the tourism sector have resulted in a wide range of benefits for the stakeholders. For example, application of ICT in the European tourism sector has played an important part in fostering interorganizational collaboration within networks of tourist destinations to develop integrated quality management practice and high competitiveness (Go and Govers 2000). In a time-series analysis across 1996–2016 evaluating around 8,000 emerging patents, digital technology in tourism is determined to be conductive to tourists and develops new tourism models (Pantano and Stylidis 2021).

Similarly, research from Australia shows that using digital tools can save small businesses in general 10 hours a week (or 0–19 employees) and boost revenue by 27% (ANZ 2018). In an analysis of 53 small and medium-sized enterprises (SMEs) in Southern England, the digital market was found to accelerate the development of tourism industry (Alford and Jones 2020). This implies that digital technology provides a good market basis for the sustainable development of tourism by shaping the destination image as well as exploring other service opportunities in cultural heritage (Gannon and Taheri 2018). For all 14 prefectures of the People's Republic of China, it has been empirically found that the digital economy is the key driving force for the high-quality development of tourism (Zhao, Mei, and Xiao 2022). The digital ecosystem of an economy empowers smart tourism by facilitating data-driven decision-making through online services, smart devices, and platforms.

The Smart Tourism Ecosystem

One important aim of this study is to examine how the digital revolution can strengthen the tourism industry. For example, digital platforms operate and facilitate travel and tourism through two segments and eight subcategories. "Direct bookings" comprise the first segment, wherein consumers purchase travel products directly from the supplier, website, or mobile application. The second segment is through indirect channels, known as online travel agencies, which are web-based marketplaces that give consumers the ability to research, compare, review, and book travel products and services from multiple suppliers simultaneously.[2] The travel and tourism subcategories are holiday packages; flights; hotels; vacation rentals; tours; activities; ride-hailing; trains, and buses; and car rentals.

A discussion of the relationship of digitalization and tourism, however, has to clarify the concepts of e-tourism, Tourism 4.0 or sometimes referred to as Hospitality Industry 4.0, and smart tourism. Gretzel et al. (2015); Pencarelli (2020); and Zeqiri, Dahmani, and Youssef (2020) usefully review key issues. This is the major component of the first strand of the framework and is detailed in Chapter 2.

Meanwhile, the generation of positive feedback loops or cycles in tourism through digitalization can be aligned with the concept of convergence. Digital convergence arises when one or more digital technologies combine to operate in a concerted fashion, allowing data and information to be shared, leading to new innovations, all of which facilitate seamless interactions across the complete journey of the tourist (OECD 2020b). In the tourism sector, convergence is occurring in two key areas: (i) the combination of digital technologies, and (ii) digital technologies merging with the physical world (e.g., wearable technologies, augmented reality, image recognition). Digital–physical convergence has spawned new hybrid products, services, and experiences.

When digital technologies are applied within innovative business models, the structure of competition, innovation, and investment can change significantly (Rachinger et al. 2019). The convergence of digital technologies creates a dynamic innovation system, which is in essence the positive feedback loop between the tourism sector and digitalization.

Expanding the Concept of Smart Tourism

Smart tourism is the evolution of traditional and e-tourism, involving technology-driven innovation and extensive adoption of ICT and the Internet of Things (IOT) (Figure 8).

Smart tourism is a step forward in the application of ICT. In this ecosystem, significant aspects of the physical and governance dimensions of tourism are digitalized, raising intelligence and efficiency. Smart tourism consists of integrated efforts at a destination to collect and aggregate or harness data from physical infrastructure and social connections, government and organizational sources, and human bodies and/or minds. Using advanced technologies, the data are consolidated and transformed into on-site experiences and business value propositions with a clear focus on efficiency, sustainability, and experience enrichment (Gretzel et al. 2015). As mentioned earlier, discussion of a smart tourism ecosystem has to clarify the concepts of e-tourism, Tourism 4.0, and smart tourism.

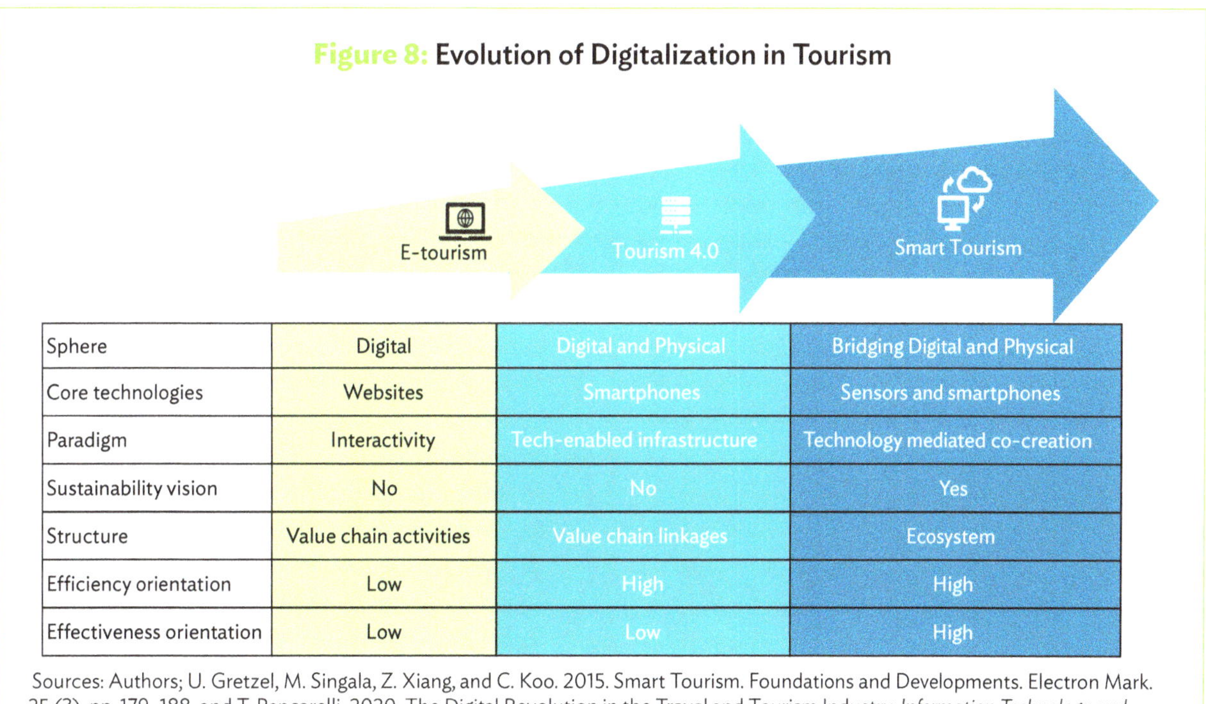

Figure 8: **Evolution of Digitalization in Tourism**

	E-tourism	Tourism 4.0	Smart Tourism
Sphere	Digital	Digital and Physical	Bridging Digital and Physical
Core technologies	Websites	Smartphones	Sensors and smartphones
Paradigm	Interactivity	Tech-enabled infrastructure	Technology mediated co-creation
Sustainability vision	No	No	Yes
Structure	Value chain activities	Value chain linkages	Ecosystem
Efficiency orientation	Low	High	High
Effectiveness orientation	Low	Low	High

Sources: Authors; U. Gretzel, M. Singala, Z. Xiang, and C. Koo. 2015. Smart Tourism. Foundations and Developments. Electron Mark. 25 (3). pp. 179–188; and T. Pencarelli. 2020. The Digital Revolution in the Travel and Tourism Industry. *Information Technology and Tourism.* 22 (3). pp. 455–476.

E-tourism

Tourism has been closely related to the evolution of ICT over the past decades. The establishment of the computer reservation systems in the 1970s, global distribution systems in the late 1980s, and the Internet in the late 1990s overhauled operational and strategic practices in the sector. Tourism information systems became a new type of business that supported e-tourism. The information extracted from these sources served as the catalyst for a variety of tasks, including dynamic packaging, travel planning, and price comparison.[3] E-tourism was a paradigm change when the application of ICT enhanced and facilitated tourism activities. It included the use of various online platforms, social media, mobile applications, and other digital tools to promote tourism products and services, manage reservations, facilitate communication between tourists and service providers, and enhance the overall tourist experience. E-tourism was mainly focused on the integration of technology with traditional tourism practices.

Tourism 4.0

Industry 4.0 ushered in a wave of digital transformation of all sectors of the global economy. New technologies and applications have been connecting individuals, organizations, and machines at unparalleled scope and speed. And this broader interaction across the physical, digital, and biological worlds has been facilitated by advances in artificial intelligence (AI), robotics, IOT, 3D printing, genetic engineering, quantum computing, big data, blockchain, and other technologies. Tourism was one of the first sectors to digitalize business processes on a global scale, bringing flight and hotel bookings online. It was therefore a natural process for Industry 4.0 to be adopted in the tourism sector.

The outcome of the Industry 4.0 adoption is Tourism 4.0, which is a more comprehensive and advanced concept that incorporates not only the use of ICT but also the aforementioned emerging technologies. It involves the digitalization and automation of various tourism processes, including personalized marketing, smart destination management, intelligent transportation, and augmented reality experiences. These technologies and their applications in the tourism industry have been elaborated upon in Appendix 2. Tourism 4.0 aims to create a more connected, immersive, and sustainable tourism experience by leveraging the latest technologies.

Smart Tourism

Smart tourism is an advanced stage of the digitalization of the sector. Smart tourism encompasses networked ICT, providing opportunities for both tourism consumers and organizations (Wang 2013). It consists of digital and virtual tourism. Information and data emanating from tourist activities, the consumption of products, and tourism and social resources can be quickly combined, thereby providing tourists, enterprises, and organizations a variety of end-user devices (Zhang 2012). With the rapid spread of mobile devices, particularly the smartphone and associated apps, an era of unprecedented connectivity and access to the Internet has been ushered in.

---

[3]   E-Tourism. https://misgempakpower.wordpress.com/e-tourism/.

Pencarelli (2020) delineates some distinguishing features of Tourism 4.0 and smart tourism. First, Tourism 4.0 is associated primarily with the new technological software and hardware, while smart tourism refers to their use in concert with human, social, and other technological resources to apply sustainability principles. Second, smart tourism gives more attention to sustainable mobility, social cohesion, protection of people's privacy, and optimization of waste management, as well as water and energy consumption in tourist locations. Third, with the use of new technologies, smart tourism subordinates normal tourism services to a vision of sustainability anchored on improving the quality of life of people—both locals and tourists—in tourism destinations.

As the sector evolved from e-tourism to Tourism 4.0 to smart tourism, the digital journey moved from a basic stage to intermediate to eventually an advanced stage. This is consistent with the stages of digitalization defined in the next section. The emergence of new information technologies, as well as the change in the buying behavior of tourists, prompted tourism managers to adopt new processes, leading to better fulfilment of all stakeholders' needs. The challenge is to make progress in digitalization consistent with the evolution from e-tourism to smart tourism.

The Various Stages of Digitalization and the Digital Divide

A digital divide in a specific population group is the unequal availability of and accessibility to digital infrastructure and technology, including smartphones, tablets, laptops, and the Internet. This results in inequality of access to information and resources. Because ICT has surpassed the manufacturing sector as the basis for faster economic growth and social mobility, people without access to ICT are at a socioeconomic disadvantage, as they are unable or less able to seek employment, buy and sell online, participate in self-governance, or undertake research and learn.

Mapping characteristics of the digital journey shows the possible stage where a country or region can be. The digital divide means that not only are different countries at different stages, but regions within countries are also at different stages. The framework for this analysis is drawn from the literature and modified for this study (Table 2).

The first stage is most important, as it forms the base for subsequent layers. In this stage, economies use computers and the Internet, but their functionality is very limited and most of the sales in the economy take place offline. The most important aspect of this stage is having the necessary infrastructure in place. In the second stage, economies use technology to provide more sophisticated digital tools. This can include use of digital platforms to provide services like e-payments, e-commerce, and digital services such as data analytics. However, major sales in the economy still take place through an offline mode. The third stage involves more advanced emerging technologies like IOT and AI, which are key components of the Fourth Industrial Revolution. The economies in this stage are capable of using advanced data analytics tools for decision-making. As a result, majority of sales take place through online channels. At this stage, countries can collaborate with each other to maximize the benefits of digital technologies. Advanced stage capabilities can enhance the potential of economic activities, including tourism.

Table 2: Stages of Digital Transformation for Any Economy

Stage	Characteristics
Basic	Telecom and infrastructure Internet usage Computer usage Web presence Offline sales
Intermediate	Digital literacy and skills Privacy and cybersecurity regulations Use of e-payments E-commerce participation Some level of data analytics used Majorly offline sales
Advanced	Creation and innovation Regional cooperation Use of the Internet of Things Use of artificial intelligence Use of software as a service/cloud-based service High usage of data analytics Majority of sales conducted online

Sources: Authors; and Institute of Southeast Asian Studies (ISEAS) – Yusof Ishak Institute. 2021. Assessing Digital Economy Policies in Six Southeast Asian. ISEAS Perspective. 50. https://www.iseas.edu.sg/wp-content/uploads/2021/03/ISEAS_Perspective_2021_50.pdf.

The digital journey can also be cast in terms of a country's or region's transition from e-tourism to smart tourism. This is directly related to the dimensions of the digital economy (Figure 9). The core of the digital economy is the ICT sector, which produces basic digital goods and services (e.g., information technology and business process management services). Together with the ICT-producing sector, the digital and platform services (e.g., Facebook and Google) comprise the digital economy in a narrow scope. The widest scope—use of ICT in all economic fields, such as automation, AI, and e-commerce, as well as the sharing economy and the gig economy—is called the "digitalized economy." Obviously, Tourism 4.0 and smart tourism are associated with the broad scope. The different stages in Table 2 can also be mapped into the three dimensions of the digital economy.

Digital Divide and Regional Cooperation

Regional cooperation aims to enhance cross-border tourism and constitutes collaboration around the digital economy. While the interaction of the tourism economy and digital transformation leads to smart tourism practices, introducing regional cooperation provides economies of scale, facilitates movement of people, and increases tourism productivity.

An integrated regional market will definitely be more productive than disjointed individual economies with inconsistent regulations. The objective is to design and implement rules and regulations that are compatible across countries, enabling local firms to operate efficiently across borders. Since no individual country is large enough to influence the structure of regulation in the digital economy, particularly in areas such as taxation and data policy, collective and coordinated action is necessary. From a wider regulatory perspective, cooperation based on a principle of openness would put any region in a much stronger position.

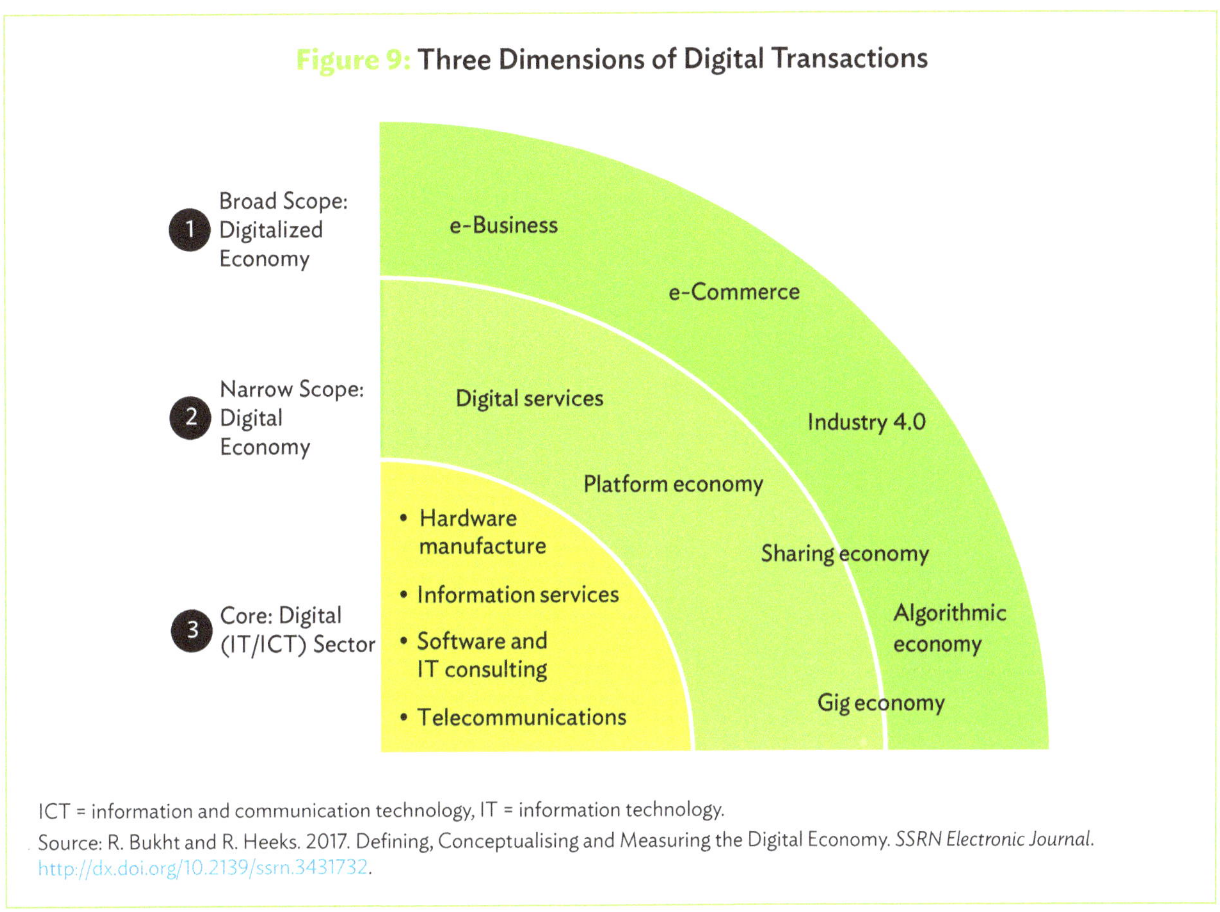

Figure 9: Three Dimensions of Digital Transactions

ICT = information and communication technology, IT = information technology.
Source: R. Bukht and R. Heeks. 2017. Defining, Conceptualising and Measuring the Digital Economy. *SSRN Electronic Journal*. http://dx.doi.org/10.2139/ssrn.3431732.

Table 3 presents an example of policies at the regional level that can deal with the issues at the heart of digitalization. Some of the policies can be initiated nationally, but areas exist that are clearly constrained by the digital divide within and between countries. This report considers both national and regional policies that can address the digital divide. These are necessary to foster a regional smart tourism ecosystem.

Table 3: Regional Issues and Possible Policy Responses

Regulatory Issue	Policy at the Regional Level
Connectivity	Cross-border connectivity including regulatory harmonization Regional compatibility of digital ID
Payments	Promoting interoperability
Logistics	Harmonized regional minimum thresholds and simplified procedures
Skills	Enabling greater regional mobility of skilled workers, including through mutual recognition of qualifications
Data policies	Pathway to regulatory coherence Open regional regime on data
Cybersecurity	Regional regulatory and enforcement collaboration including overarching governance framework

Source: World Bank. 2019. *The Digital Economy in Southeast Asia: Strengthening the Foundations for Future Growth*. Washington, DC.

Meanwhile, a tourism value chain integrated regionally should experience similar benefits. Facilitating travel into, around, and between the countries of a particular region can significantly increase profitability. Given that the essence of tourism is to create and foster better dialogue, increased people-to-people exchanges, more economic ties, and increased connectivity throughout a particular region, its development should be an operational priority under various regional groupings. This report raises the possibility that the tourism sector can be a laboratory to demonstrate the need for collective action in digitalization. This is related to its possible role as a focal point of regional cooperation in digitalization.

Sample of Policy Recommendations

Digital development has transformed smart tourism by empowering travelers with information, convenience, personalization, and immersive experiences, thereby enabling smart destinations and smart travel. It provides tourists end-to-end assistance from trip planning, booking, and reservations using targeted recommendations. On the supply side, businesses can adapt and offer innovative services with the help of big data analytics to make data-driven decisions for higher personalization. However, there are gaps and challenges largely emanating from the digital divide that constrain the progress of digitalization in the tourism sector and the economy as a whole. Table 3 gives a succinct presentation of the type of policy recommendations that can overcome these gaps and challenges. This chapter enumerates a sample of these policies at the regional level that are discussed in full in Chapter 5.

Cryptography: Governments should encourage collaboration with technology experts, researchers, and cryptographic communities to ensure encryption algorithms remain secure against emerging threats.

Intellectual property, source code: Regional groupings should enable member nations to create necessary regulatory frameworks to enforce and uphold nondisclosure agreements between parties involved in the development, distribution, or licensing of source code.

Consumer protection: Regional cooperation mechanisms should adopt a multistakeholder approach and collaborate with industrial, government, and global stakeholders to address issues affecting online safety and security. As an illustration, governments should adhere to guidelines released by international agencies, such as the "Consumer Protection in E-Commerce" by the OECD (2016) and the "Consumers International Guidelines for Online Product Safety" by Consumers International (2021).

Digital identities: The most critical element in this regard is harmonization of digital ID standards. For example, the "Catalogue of Technical Standards for Digital Identification Systems," developed by the World Bank (Mittal 2022), provides standards for different types of digital identities.

Data sharing: Regional groupings should encourage member countries to establish clear policies and guidelines that promote the release of government data in open and machine-readable formats.

Quality of service: Regional groupings should encourage governments to adopt internationally recognized standards in the digital economy, like the "United Nations Commission on International Trade Law (UNCITRAL) Model Law on Electronic Commerce" by the United Nations (1999) and the World Trade Organization's rules and principles on digital trade.

Artificial intelligence: Regional groupings should encourage member countries to establish regulatory frameworks that address the unique challenges posed by AI and emerging technologies. These frameworks should guide the development, deployment, and use of AI systems.

2 The Smart Tourism Ecosystem

This chapter extends the discussion of smart tourism and shows how the tourism value chain can be aligned to the smart tourism ecosystem. Two concepts underpin the tourism value chain: the four principles of smart tourism and its two components. Their interaction expands the framework presented in Figure 5 and forms the main structure of the report. How far the tools and technology of the Fourth Industrial Revolution can support the smart tourism ecosystem is the major theme of this chapter. Case studies are presented to strengthen the argument that the entire tourism value chain can be digitally enhanced.

Principles of Smart Tourism

Smart tourism can be conceptualized using four principles: attractiveness, accessibility, sustainability, and collaborative partnership (Figure 10).

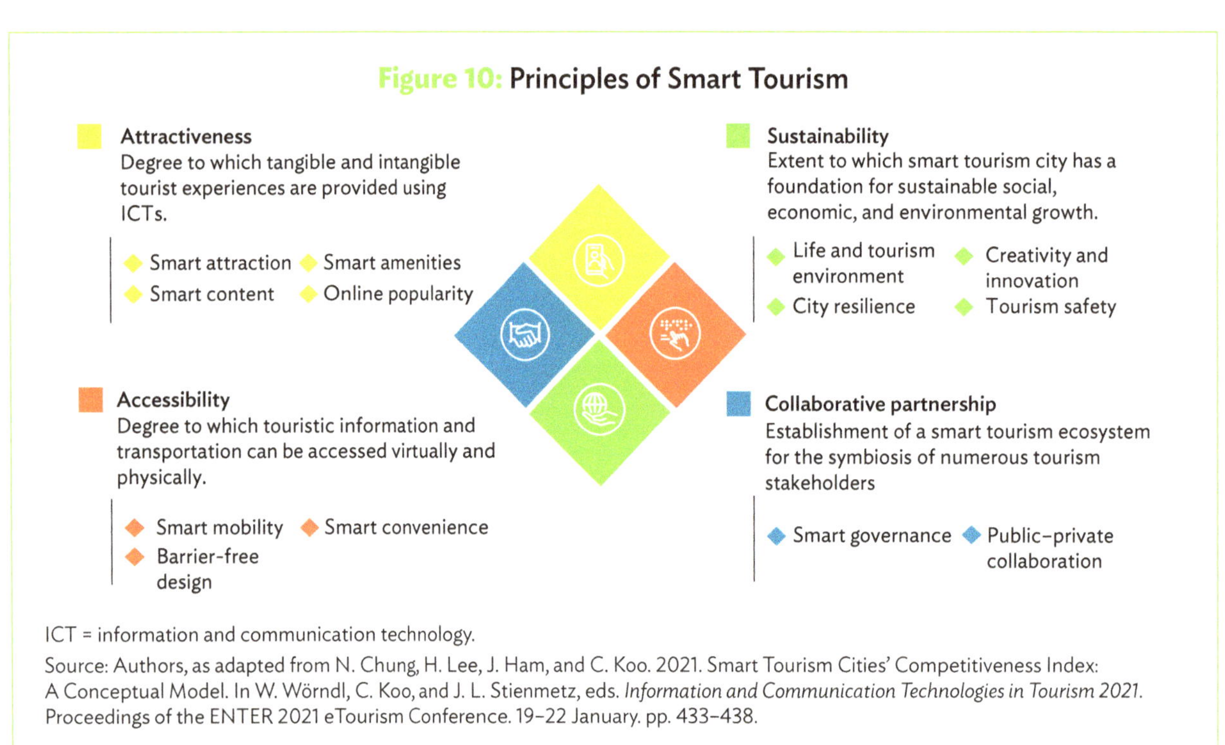

Figure 10: Principles of Smart Tourism

ICT = information and communication technology.
Source: Authors, as adapted from N. Chung, H. Lee, J. Ham, and C. Koo. 2021. Smart Tourism Cities' Competitiveness Index: A Conceptual Model. In W. Wörndl, C. Koo, and J. L. Stienmetz, eds. *Information and Communication Technologies in Tourism 2021*. Proceedings of the ENTER 2021 eTourism Conference. 19–22 January. pp. 433–438.

(i)   **Attractiveness.** The use of advanced technologies from the Fourth Industrial Revolution can enhance the attractiveness of tourist destinations, experiences, and services. These technologies can be used to provide personalized and interactive experiences for tourists, enable real-time information and recommendations, facilitate seamless transactions and communication, and improve overall efficiency and sustainability of tourism operations. They include smart content, smart attraction, smart amenities, and online popularity (Chung et al. 2021).

(ii)   **Accessibility.** Accessibility in smart tourism refers to the use of advanced technologies and design principles to create inclusive and accessible tourism experiences for people with disabilities, seniors, and others with specific needs. The outcome is smart mobility, smart convenience, and barrier-free designs (Chung et al. 2021). In essence, accessible tourism enables people with access requirements to function independently and with equality and dignity through the delivery of universally designed tourism products, services, and environments (Darcy and Dickson 2009). This can include providing real-time information about accessibility features of tourist destinations, such as wheelchair ramps, accessible toilets, and audio guides for the visually impaired. Smart tourism can also improve accessibility in booking processes and communication, including online reservation systems that cater to specific needs, and the provision of multilingual assistance and services for international visitors.

(iii)   **Sustainability.** This principle is currently the most relevant as it determines the extent to which the smart tourism city or place has a foundation for sustainable social, economic, and environmental growth. This can manifest in the form of resilience, tourist safety, creativity and innovation, and life and tourism environment (Chung et al. 2021). It can also include the use of renewable energy sources, smart building designs, and waste management systems to reduce the environmental impact of tourism activities. The promotion of responsible tourism practices, such as reducing carbon emissions, protecting biodiversity, and supporting local communities is part of environmental sustainability. Smart tourism can also enhance social sustainability by promoting cultural exchange, creating job opportunities, and improving the overall quality of life for residents. Additionally, smart tourism can help improve the economic sustainability of tourism businesses by enhancing their competitiveness and reducing their operating costs.

(iv)   **Collaborative partnership.** The main channels are public–private collaboration and smart governance (Chung et al. 2021). Collaborative partnerships allow sharing of resources, knowledge, and expertise to improve the overall quality of tourism services and enhance the visitor experience. For example, public–private partnerships (PPPs) can be used to develop smart city infrastructure that can support smart tourism. Key aspects of a smart city include intelligent transportation systems, smart lighting, and waste management systems. Collaboration between tourism businesses and technology providers can lead to the development of innovative and personalized tourism products and services. Meanwhile, collaborative partnerships also play a critical role in ensuring the sustainable development of tourism, by involving local communities and promoting their participation in tourism planning and decision-making (Graci 2020). This approach can lead to more inclusive and sustainable tourism development that benefits both visitors and local residents.

Components of Smart Tourism

Smart tourism consists of two major components, smart travel and smart destination (Figure 11), both of which aggregate the elements of the tourism value chain (as discussed in Chapter 1). Travel covers all the services and activities related to getting the tourist from origin to destination.[4] Meanwhile, a smart destination facilitates access to tourism and hospitality products, services, spaces, and experiences through ICT-based tools, increasing the tourist's satisfaction. The transportation element is part of both components as it covers both air travel and other domestic travel modes.

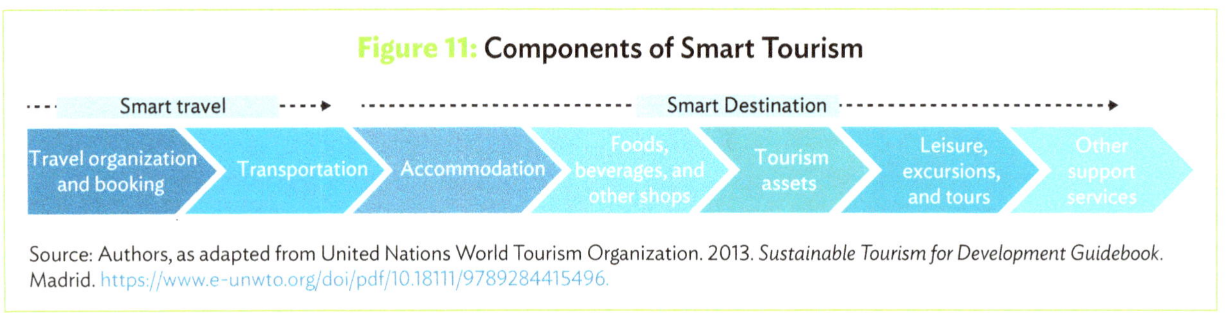

Figure 11: Components of Smart Tourism

Source: Authors, as adapted from United Nations World Tourism Organization. 2013. *Sustainable Tourism for Development Guidebook.* Madrid. https://www.e-unwto.org/doi/pdf/10.18111/9789284415496.

Smart Travel

UNWTO defines the smart travel model as one that includes smart visas, borders, security processes, and infrastructure.[5] The World Economic Forum (WEF) identifies two main factors for smart travel: (i) visa processes and the airport experience (WEF 2014). The OECD identifies four areas for seamless travel: visa requirement and acquisition; (ii) digital traveler identity and biometrics; (iii) multimodal transport and connectivity; and (iv) visitor handling, information, and management (OECD 2020c). The World Travel and Tourism Council defines seamless travel as a journey where a traveler does not have to present travel-related documents to multiple stakeholders at multiple checkpoints (WTTC 2020). Based on the above review, smart travel can be defined as "Making the journey of traveler between the origin and the destination easier, more efficient, and more pleasant for the passengers with the help of technology, while maintaining high levels of safety and security."

A tourist's journey consists of many steps, starting from planning the trip to entering the destination country. However, there are certain steps that become bottlenecks for the customer journey. First is visa application and screening process. The uncertainty about visa requirements, the need to share numerous documents with embassies, and the lack of integration of digital identities make the process inefficient and time-consuming. The second step is the booking processes, where the tourist needs to provide the same information to multiple stakeholders. Third is check-in processes, where manual inspection of documents can impact the efficiency of operations. Fourth is security checkpoints, which again are impacted by capacity constraints and resource-intensive screening processes arising from lack of passenger information. Fifth is the airport experience, which includes navigation across the

---

4   Association of Caribbean States. Travel Facilitation Key to Tourism Development. http://www.acs-aec.org/index. php?q=sustainable-tourism/travel-facilitation-key-to-tourism-development.

5   For more information, see UNWTO. Digital Transformation. https://www.unwto.org/digital-transformation.

airport, interaction with stakeholders, departure gate, and exit control. Last step is the border security, where passengers might have to face long queues for the immigration process (WEF 2018).

The relevant principles of smart tourism can be applied to each of the journey steps mentioned above. Table 4 shows the relevance of smart tourism principles and subpillars for each step. Some subpillars, such as smart attractions, are not applicable for smart travel and, hence, are not included here.

Table 4: Application of Principles of Smart Tourism to the Travel Component

Principles of Smart Tourism		Attractiveness		Accessibility		Sustainability	Collaborative Partnership	
Subpillars		**Smart Content**	**Smart Amenities**	**Barrier-Free Designs**	**Smart Convenience**	**Tourism Safety**	**Smart Governance**	**Public–Private Collaboration**
Pre-trip	**Booking**	Clean and simple interface			Multiple language support			Incorporating digital identity into existing processes
	Permission to travel	Clean and simple visa process			Multiple language support	Data protection	Standardized global protocols	Effective data sharing between countries
Departure	**Check-in**			Disability assistance	Minimal waiting time	Contactless check-in	Standardized global protocols	
	Security checks			Disability assistance	Minimal waiting time	Contact-less security checks	Standardized global protocols	
	Airport experience		Smart baggage handling, free Wi-Fi	Disability assistance	Smart navigation systems			Digital identity wallets to provide necessary verification (ID, age, etc.)
Arrival	**Border crossing**			Disability assistance	Minimal waiting time	Contactless process	Standardized global protocols	Effective data sharing between countries

Sources: Authors; World Economic Forum. 2014. *Smart Travel – Unlocking Economic Growth and Development through Travel Facilitation.* Geneva; and World Travel and Tourism Council. 2019. *Visa Facilitation: Enabling Travel and Job Creation through Secure and Seamless Cross-Border Travel.* London.

Significant technological advances, especially in biometrics, have produced digital solutions that enable identity verification, creating a frictionless journey, improving security, strengthening health safety, and promoting commercial benefits. The World Travel and Tourism Council's vision of safe and seamless travel promotes use of biometrics and digital identities across each stage. Use of digital identities can stimulate tourism demand post pandemic because of the inclusion of health and safety components. At the global level, the aviation sector benefits $18 per dollar investment made, by using digital identities for the sector. Apart from economic benefits, digital identities also improve safety and security of the whole process by providing accurate confirmation of a passenger's identity. It also addresses health concerns due to the contactless process (WTTC 2020).

Owing to the technologies utilized along the value chain, a lot of data are collected that can be transformed into big data using modern techniques and algorithms. Moreover, supervised learning can also be applied on big data to create knowledge patterns and sentiment analysis. The results can help destination management organizations, tourism agencies, governments, and SMEs to tweak their business models for higher tourist satisfaction, raising profits.

Smart Destination

A smart tourist destination takes inspiration from all the principles of smart tourism (Figure 12). The smart tourism destination stands firm on the foundation of higher accessibility (through smart convenience and barrier-free design), higher attractiveness (through smart content and smart amenities), and backing of strong collaborative partnership (through secure networks and apps) between tourism service providers and the government. This helps provide a memorable and holistic experience to the tourist without harm to environmental resources and social disturbance, creating sustainability and resilience in the tourism environment.

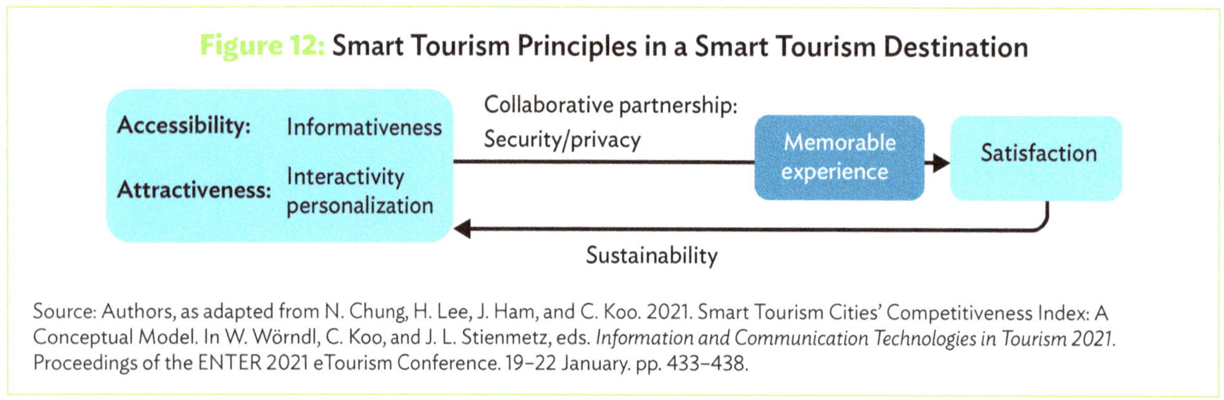

Figure 12: Smart Tourism Principles in a Smart Tourism Destination

Source: Authors, as adapted from N. Chung, H. Lee, J. Ham, and C. Koo. 2021. Smart Tourism Cities' Competitiveness Index: A Conceptual Model. In W. Wörndl, C. Koo, and J. L. Stienmetz, eds. *Information and Communication Technologies in Tourism 2021.* Proceedings of the ENTER 2021 eTourism Conference. 19–22 January. pp. 433–438.

This integrated platform has multiple touch points that could be accessed through a variety of end-user devices. These will then create and facilitate real-time tourism experiences and improve the effectiveness of tourism resources management throughout the destination at both the micro and macro level (Buhalis and Amaranggana 2013). According to the conceptual model for smart tourism destinations, there are five layers (Figure 13):

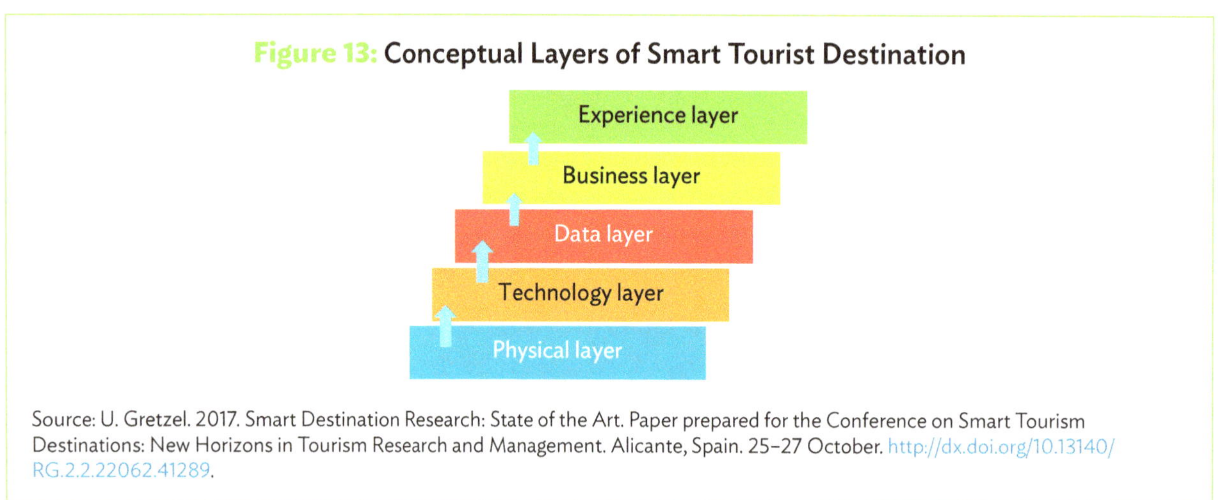

Figure 13: Conceptual Layers of Smart Tourist Destination

Source: U. Gretzel. 2017. Smart Destination Research: State of the Art. Paper prepared for the Conference on Smart Tourism Destinations: New Horizons in Tourism Research and Management. Alicante, Spain. 25–27 October. http://dx.doi.org/10.13140/RG.2.2.22062.41289.

These layers can operate in an efficient and effective manner through the collaborative partnership of all tourism sector stakeholders. Three areas of such collaborative partnership are discussed below.

(i) **Destination management organizations**

Destination management calls for a coalition of many organizations and interests working toward a common goal: ensuring the competitiveness and sustainability of the tourism destination. Though destination management organizations have typically undertaken marketing activities, their remit is becoming far broader, to become a strategic leader in destination development.[6] These organizations take advantage of the destination's unique potential by conducting market research, implementing destination marketing strategies, and attracting investment. The Korea Tourism Organization is one such global public enterprise, which promotes the Republic of Korea as a world-class travel destination. The organization aims to improve quality of life in the country and spread Korean culture worldwide through the strengthening and development of the tourism industry (Box 1).

Box 1: Korea Tourism Organization

Webpage: Korea Everywhere GusukGusuk (http://korean.visit korea.or.kr)

- 10 language services provided at the portal.
- KTO sets marketing strategies by understanding foreign users' behavior demands.
- Offering: Users can collect practical tour products and information, or select virtual tour guide for travelers in only specific sites, famous historical destination, museums, trails, mainly with storytelling information using smart phone's audio service and AR.
- KTO's domestic webpage recorded 680,000 page views in a day.

Social Network Service: Facebook (Korea Everywhere Live), Twitter (@Kor_Visitkorea)

- Acts as bridge to KTO webpage for the users who want more details.
- More than 50,000 users click in KTO's Facebook page and about 470 people are using actively (2011).
- As for the overseas SNS service, one or more channels are operated to give tourism information for foreign travelers, especially Korean wave.

GusukGusuk App (Korea Everywhere App)

- Domestic app "Korea Everywhere" emphasizes where to go travel (for inbound tourists).
- English app "Visit Korea" tells on how to travel for outbound tourists.
- Korea Everywhere and Visit Korea applications have been downloaded by 2.37 million users (Korea Everywhere: 2.15 million, Visit Korea: 0.22 million).
- Awarded the grand prize in IT department of information culture prize in 2012.

AR = augmented reality, IT = information technology, KTO = Korea Tourist Organization.

Sources: Study team analysis of individual websites and social media sites; and Visit Korea. https://english.visitkorea.or.kr/enu/index.kto.

---

6   UNWTO. Policy and Destination Management. https://www.unwto.org/policy-destination-management.

(ii) Private sector

PPPs are essential for managing smart tourism destination initiatives. They foster efficiency, creativity, and innovation (Heeley 2011). Private companies innovate design and share project management skills and risk management know-how.

(iii) Trusted third parties

Through tourism information systems, smart tourism destinations capture information about users and their activities that could be deeply personal, including their physical location, and thus may infringe privacy. Hiring a trusted third party is one solution to conceal users' real identities. Since most destinations use video surveillance systems to supply real-time information on public transportation and traffic situations, a trusted third party could take advantage of several users being in the same location to cloak their actual locations (Buhalis and Amaranggana 2013).

Smart Tools to Facilitate Smart Tourism

Technology is at the core of the smart tourism concept and it must be leveraged appropriately to improve tourism services. The delivery of tourism services is coursed through a multitude of technologies emanating from the Fourth Industrial Revolution technologies. For tourists, these technologies are associated with a set of smart tools (Figure 14).

Figure 14: Smart Tools for Tourism Industry

Smart Identity

Smart identity is a replacement of a paper-based ID, which can be authenticated remotely over digital channels.

Smart Platforms

Digital platforms are digital services that facilitate interaction between two or more distinct but independent sets of users via the Internet.

Smart Logistics

Smart logistics refers to the use of advanced technologies to coordinate movement of people, goods, and vehicles from one place to another.

Smart Experience

Smart experiencing is enhancing tourist experience using technology through different media like audio, visual, etc.

Smart Devices

Smart device is a context-aware electronic device capable of performing autonomous computing and connecting to other devices, either with wire or wirelessly, for data exchange.

Sources: Authors; McKinsey Global Institute. 2019. *Digital Identification: A Key to Inclusive Growth.* https://www.mckinsey.com/capabilities/mckinsey-digital/our-insights/digital-identification-a-key-to-inclusive-growth; Organisation for Economic Co-operation and Development. 2019. *An Introduction to Online Platforms and Their Role in the Digital Transformation.* Paris: OECD Publishing. https://doi.org/10.1787/53e5f593-en; and M. Silverio-Fernández, S. Renukappa, and S. Suresh. 2018. What Is a Smart Device? A Conceptualisation within the Paradigm of the Internet of Things. *Visualization in Engineering.* 6 (1). 3. http://dx.doi.org/10.1186/s40327-018-0063-8.

One important thing to note is that these tools are neither technology-specific nor can any technology be associated with a single smart tool. For example, cloud computing delivers computing services, including servers, database, storage, networking, etc., over the Internet.[7] However, it cannot be associated with a single tool mentioned above. It could be a part of every tool based on the application. These tools can be used to enhance the tourist experience across the smart tourism components (smart travel and smart destination). Figure 15 shows the application of these tools across the elements of the value chain.

Figure 15: Application of Smart Tools across Tourism Value Chain

Smart Tools	Smart Travel Facilitation		Smart Tourist Destination			
	Travel organization and booking	Transportation	Accommodation	Foods, beverages, and other shops	Tourism assets	Leisure, excursions, and tours
Smart Identity	Automated check in, smart visas, health certificates	Tourist passes, facial verification	Automated check-in and check-out	Thermal screening	Thermal screening, tourist passes	Thermal screening, tourist passes
Smart Platforms	Aggregators, marketing, chatbots, payment system	Sharing economy, aggregators, payment system	Sharing economy, aggregators, payment system	Online ordering, reservations, reviews and ratings, payment system	Information dissemination, ticket booking, payment system	Information dissemination, ticket booking, payment system
Smart Logistics	Smart baggage management	Integrated traffic management, autonomous vehicles	Smart baggage management	Food delivery systems	Crowd management	Crowd management
Smart Experience	...	...	Virtual tours	Interactive menus	Virtual tours, metaverse	Virtual tours, metaverse
Smart Devices	...	Baggage tracking, fleet management	Smart rooms	Inventory management	Smart sensors for tracking	Personalized experience

... = not applicable.

Note: This table is illustrative and nonexhaustive.

Source: Authors' illustration.

Smart tools are applications of digital technologies that can significantly impact traveler numbers and behavior by enhancing their overall travel experience and addressing various pain points in the journey. Innovations in the elements of the tourism value chain make tourism more attractive, and contactless travel experiences and smart platforms with real-time information make it more accessible. Additionally, these smart tools have created a dynamic ecosystem to promote a responsible and sustainable travel industry through green destinations, energy-efficient modes of transport, sustainable certification and badges, and carbon footprint calculators for tourists. By leveraging technology, data, and user engagement, smart tools can drive collaboration among travelers, businesses, and governments through real-time data sharing, digital authentication, smart

---

[7]   Azure. What Is Cloud Computing? A Beginner's Guide. https://azure.microsoft.com/en-us/resources/cloud-computing-dictionary/what-is-cloud-computing.

passes, and online applications to enable interaction with locals. Recently, a strong correlation has been found between the growth of tourism and environmental impacts, such as loss of natural resources and biodiversity (Kim, Lee, and Kim 2020). Some destinations have taken this further and introduced restrictions on the number of tourists at a given time, with examples of this increasing around the world. How can digitalization help?

On the one hand, digital applications can influence a change in travel volume. This refers to changes in the number of trips as well as distance covered and number of days away. An increase in travel volume generally constitutes more of a risk than an opportunity for sustainable tourism development.

On the other hand, digital applications can influence changes to travel behavior. This refers to how travelers organize their trip, such as mobility (choice of transport to and from the destination and at the destination), accommodation (type and category), and organization of stay (such as type and number of points of interest visited).

Case Studies of Smart Tools Used in the Tourism Industry

DigiYatra: Contactless Check-In Process Using Biometrics

This case study illustrates how use of digital identities (smart identity) and mobile applications (smart platforms) can facilitate smart travel by improving efficiency and making the overall process more secure (Figure 16). Smart tourism principles touch on attractiveness (smart content), accessibility (smart convenience and smart mobility), sustainability (tourism safety), and collaborative partnerships (smart governance and public–private collaboration).

DigiYatra is an Indian platform, which aims to facilitate contactless passenger identification at the airport using facial recognition technology. The initiative aims to make the passenger journey easy and simple, reduce operational costs, digitize current manual processes, and improve efficiency while enhancing security standards. The DigiYatra app is available on almost all smart devices, such as Android and iPhone Operating System (iOS) phones, where users have to register using a mobile number. Users then need to link their government IDs with their profile. In this case, users can either link India's government ID—Aadhaar through DigiLocker or through offline mode. DigiLocker is a platform for providing issuance and verification of documents digitally. After uploading own image on the platform, the passenger can use the app to check-in at the airport easily with the steps illustrated in Figure 16:

Figure 16: Steps to Use DigiYatra

Scan the boarding pass onDigiYatra app at the departure gate

Look into the camera and get the face scanned

The gates will open automatically and let passenger enter inside

Source: New Delhi Airport. DigiYatra: A Contactless Air Travel Solution. https://www.newdelhiairport.in/digiyatra.

This process has multiple benefits. The passenger does not need to show the boarding pass or ID at multiple checkpoints. The human intervention and waiting time along the process is minimized. Additionally, availability of real-time information on passenger load can lead to better resource planning.[8]

Seamless Travel Experience through Mobility-as-a-Service in European Cities

This case study illustrates how few tourist destinations are enhancing the travel experience of tourists within cities with smart mobility services with the help of mobile applications (smart platforms) and real-time monitoring (smart logistics). In smart tourism principles, it touches on attractiveness (smart content and smart amenities), accessibility (smart convenience and smart mobility), sustainability (creativity and innovation), and collaborative partnerships (smart governance and public–private collaboration).

The United Nations defines Mobility-as-a-Service (MaaS) as "a user-centric transportation management system, using intelligent mobility distribution systems and IOT applications, in which all transport modes service operators and infrastructure providers are connected under a single platform, which supplies mobility options to travelers, providing real-time traffic information, service conditions, and operator arrangements, and delivering online ticketing and payment options" (UNECE 2020). The service integrates all of a destination's means of transport, like public transport, taxis, vehicle hires, bicycles, etc., through a single service provider via a mobile app. Service providers in Europe include Whim in Helsinki, WienMobil in Vienna, and Mobilitatsshop in Hanover, among others.

Critical issues affecting travel in cities include inefficient management of tourist mobility, overcrowding of public places, and lack of measures to reduce the ecological footprint of the entire travel ecosystem. MaaS tackles these issues with the use of geolocation technology and effective use of the mobile platform. The platform can design the optimal path of travel between two points as it has access to all transport modes available, both public and private. This helps provide last-mile connectivity by offering alternative means of transport. The platform also provides integrated payment solutions. From the user's perspective, the service has five different levels depending on the degree of integration of travel services.

(i)   Level 1 means there is no integration at all. Different service providers have different modes of operations, and the traveler needs to plan his journey manually.
(ii)   Level 2 includes integration of just information on travel services into one interface. This allows the traveler to search for routes and modes of transport at a given time of the day.
(iii)   Level 3 builds upon the previous level and allows the traveler to find, book, and pay for the trip entirely through a single app. For example, moovel or moovit in Germany allow multimodal ticketing in multiple cities. The passengers can book tickets on Germany's national train service, Deutsche Bahn, and can cover the rest of the journey with car or bike sharing.

---

[8]   Delhi Airport. DigiYatra: A Contactless Air Travel Solution. https://www.newdelhiairport.in/digiyatra; and India.gov.in. Digi Yatra–A New Digital Experience for Air Travellers. https://www.india.gov.in/spotlight/digi-yatra-new-digital-experience-air-travellers.

(iv)   Level 4 builds upon the previous level by adding an additional service of subscription packages. These packages have a fixed time period like a month or week. For example, Whim app in Helsinki provides different monthly packages which allow discounted taxi rides, car rentals, etc. across the city.

(v)   Level 5 goes beyond the link of supply and demand for mobility. This level also takes societal and economic objectives into account, like encouraging most virtuous means of transport. This level requires involvement of public authorities of cities in terms of preparing suitable public policies, providing incentives, etc.

The MaaS service is beneficial to multiple stakeholders. For travelers, it provides integrated and easily accessible travel options to explore the destination. Businesses can identify new markets and new business opportunities. The actual transport operators benefit from reduced operational cost. The public sector can benefit from creation of new jobs, increased efficiency, and improved reliability of transport systems. Some of the studies on the impact of MaaS in Europe have provided positive results. In Vienna, users of MaaS system showed a reduction in car use by 21% and increase in public transport and taxis by 26%. In Helsinki, a survey conducted in 2018 showed that MaaS users make more frequent use of public transport and taxis than the average population.[9]

SmartGates at Australian Airports

This case study is a good example of how digital identities (smart identity) can be used to make the immigration process more efficient and secure. In terms of smart tourism principles, it touches upon attractiveness (smart convenience and barrier-free design), sustainability (tourism safety), and collaborative partnerships (smart governance and public–private collaboration).

SmartGate is an automated self-service border control system operated by the Australian Border Force and New Zealand Customs Service. SmartGates are installed at immigration checkpoints in departure and arrival halls in 10 international airports in Australia and 4 New Zealand international airports. These allow Australian electronic Passport (ePassport) holders and ePassport holders of a number of other countries to clear immigration controls more rapidly and ensure travel security. SmartGates use facial recognition technology and ePassports to validate the identity of passengers, allowing faster and smoother operations. The service is provided in over 20 languages and the design of SmartGates can accommodate wheelchairs. Upon arrival at the airport, a traveler needs to fill in details on a passenger card, which would help them in going through the SmartGate. The step-by-step process flow is outlined in Figure 17.

9   Cerema. 2019. *MaaS in Europe: Lessons from the Helsinki, Vienna and Hanover Experiments.* https://www.cerema.fr/system/files/documents/2020/04/cerema_parangonnage_maas_synthesis_eng.pdf; United Nations Economic Commission for Europe, Inland Transport Committee. 2020. *Transport Trends and Economics 2018–2019: Mobility as a Service.* Geneva. https://unece.org/DAM/trans/main/wp5/publications/Mobility_as_a_Service_Transport_Trends_and_Economics_2018-2019.pdf; and Segittur (State Company for the Management of Tourism Innovation and Technologies). 2021. Guide for Best Practices in Digitalisation for Smart Destinations. Press release. 11 November.

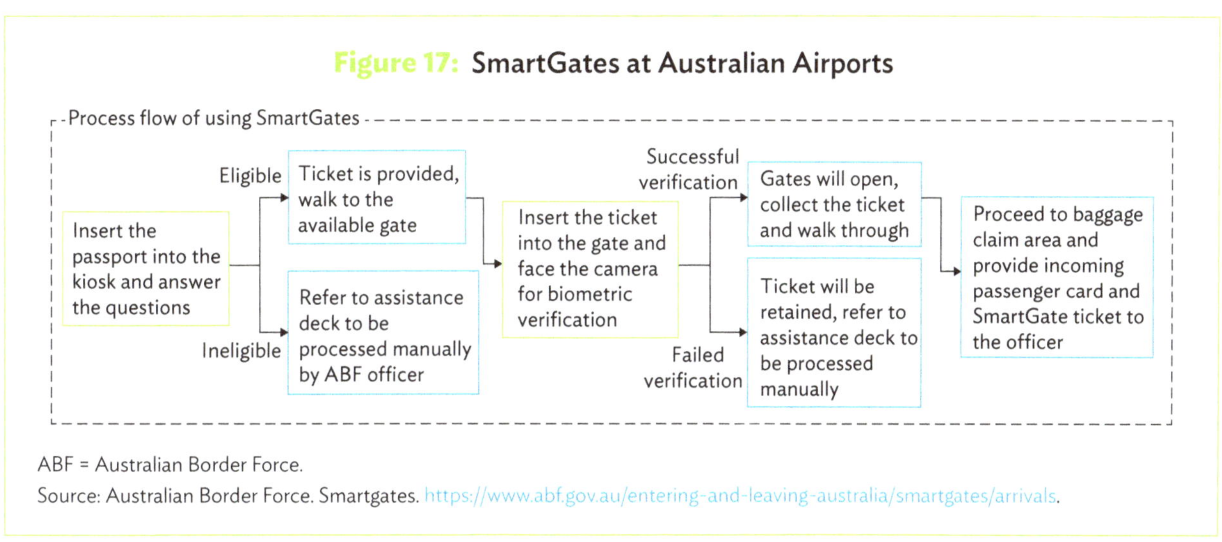

ABF = Australian Border Force.
Source: Australian Border Force. Smartgates. https://www.abf.gov.au/entering-and-leaving-australia/smartgates/arrivals.

As a result of this self-service procedure, smart convenience and barrier-free design ensure higher accessibility. Not only this, by using biometric information backed by federal privacy laws, tourism safety is taken care of. Finally, the verification of biometric information is carried through strong, well-enforced public–private collaboration.

Smart Tourist Experiences in Europe

This case study is a collection of three different examples on how technology can be used in smart destinations to provide a unique experience. It illustrates how augmented and virtual (smart experience) reality technologies are being used in the tourism industry and how mobile applications (smart platforms) can provide a unique travel experience. In smart tourism principles, this case study touches on attractiveness (smart attraction and smart content) and sustainability (creativity and innovation).

Many European smart destinations use AI and augmented and virtual reality technologies to enhance the tourist experience and provide a realistic feel of the past, present, and future. Among the applications of augmented and virtual reality in tourism with the most potential are virtual reality travel, virtual hotel tours, immersive navigation and guided tours, test drive excursions, enhanced museum experience, and gamified tours. A few examples of such experiences are

(i)   Virtual reality experience at the Berlin Wall Memorial in Germany: This lets visitors step back in time to experience what life was like during the Cold War and the construction and fall of the Berlin Wall. The German tech start-up TimeRide offers an incredibly immersive bus tour across Berlin landmarks using VR goggles.[10]

(ii) Augmented reality art application in Valencia, Spain: This augmented reality application allows users to interact with the ninot painting of the artist Ramón Solaz, which can be visited at the Ninot Exhibition. The ninot symbolizes a neuron, which forms part of a virtual brain. The user can explore it through the mobile application to obtain information about the latest discoveries

---

[10]   European Union. Explore the Berlin Wall as it Stood, in Virtual Reality. https://www.themayor.eu/en/a/view/explore-the-berlin-wall-as-it-stood-in-virtual-reality-3667.

on the field of neuroscience. The augmented reality application can be installed on numerous operating systems and can identify several types of neurons (European Commission 2022).

(iii)   Tourist touring app in Athens, Greece "Narratologies": This is a location-based app having a city exploration game in the city offering alternative, self-guided city exploration and shopping tours.[11] The app creates a hybrid experience of urban cultural exploration by utilizing gamification techniques combined with location intelligence. The app guides visitors independently and at their own pace around the city while exploring hidden stories and acquiring unique rewards from local businesses, providing the user with an exciting way to experience Athens off the beaten track (European Commission 2022).

Crowd Management through IOT Sensors in Barcelona

A large group of tourists can be effectively managed with IOT sensors (smart devices). Among the smart tourism principles, this case study touches on accessibility (smart mobility), sustainability (tourism safety, and creativity and innovation), and collaborative partnerships (smart governance and public–private collaboration).

Crowd management refers to managing a large group of people at a certain destination. It is particularly important in the tourism sector to regularly monitor the number of tourists entering the destination and to track the movement of people. A public–private collaboration between Mobile World Capital Barcelona and local network operator Orange has been working to monitor the number of tourists visiting Sagrada Familia in Barcelona, a major tourist destination in the city.

The tourist site realized that, although many tourists were visiting the site, only few of them were paying to enter the Sagrada Familia. Many of the tourists remained outside the cathedral. Barcelona City officials wanted to track tourists accurately so that they could plan transport networks accordingly and encourage more travelers to enter the site. The project used different IOT sensors to analyze tourists' data. The sensors included

- nine wireless fidelity (Wi-Fi) sensors to analyze traveler flow and their movement around the area,
- one Global System for Mobile Communication (GSM) sensor to obtain the nationality of the traveler, and
- three 3D sensors to count the number of people entering and exiting from the metro stations.

These sensors allowed collection of detailed data, and its analysis provided more accurate insights into points such as street activity, the flow of people, country origin of traveler, gender, age range, tourist visit length, and hourly distribution, etc. (Ajuntament de Barcelona, n.d.). The initiative enabled the city to understand how tourists move around, including the places they are staying at and other tourist destinations they visited. Local authorities used the insights to set up ticket booths at appropriate locations and increase "footfall" at Sagrada Familia and to take measures to better accommodate and transport the travelers in the city (GSMA 2016).

---

[11]   Narratologies app, https://narratologies.com/.

Conclusion

The case studies show the extensive coverage of the smart tourism ecosystem. The tools and technologies of the Fourth Industrial Revolution have deeply permeated the tourism value chain and heavily support the four principles of smart tourism and its two components. However, it remains to be seen if they can be scaled up both *within* countries and *across* countries. Countries, or even regions within a country, differ in their level of digitalization and in progress in transitioning from e-tourism to smart tourism. The next chapter looks at the digital divide, how it is affected by a country's level of development, and how it impacts smart tourism ecosystem progress. This lays the groundwork for the role of regional cooperation.

3

Varying Country Readiness for Smart Tourism

Smart tourism seems to be the future. Building on the previous case studies , this chapter details and analyzes the principles of smart tourism to reveal levers or parameters policymakers can build on and navigate. Meanwhile, quantitative measure of a country's performance on the principles can guide policymakers on country readiness to adopt smart travel and smart destination practices. Importantly, countries should deepen digitalization transition from e-tourism to smart tourism.

Objective for Assessing Countries' Readiness for Smart Tourism

Chapter 2 of this report presented the main framework underlying the discussion. The four principles and corresponding subprinciples of smart tourism are an important component that provide a pathway for countries to develop smart travel and tourist attractions as smart destinations. By comparing the performance of countries on these principles and subprinciples, readiness to operate in the smart tourism ecosystem can be assessed. This will help policymakers recognize best practices and enable them to craft strategies and policies aligned to their countries' circumstances and objectives.

As a specific case study, this chapter focuses on Southeast Asia, that is, selected ASEAN countries. Performance of selected countries is analyzed and compared on the subprinciples of smart tourism. Apart from being part of Asia and the Pacific region, ASEAN countries have adopted a tourism strategy both at national and regional levels consistent with the theme of this report. As a region, the countries have recognized the value of a "quality sustainable tourism destination, which promotes the economic prosperity, welfare, and engagement of local community; protects and develops its natural environment and culture; and provides a high-quality experience to responsible and sustainable minded visitors or tourists" (ERIA 2022). To pursue this vision, ASEAN leaders adopted the Declaration on Digital Tourism on 12 November 2020.[12] In particular, leaders encouraged "the development of a dynamic, competitive, creative, and synchronized ASEAN tourism industry, through digital transformation, to accelerate economic growth and social advancement" (ASEAN 2020).

---

[12]   For more information, see ASEAN Declaration on Digital Tourism. https://asean.org/wp-content/uploads/2021/09/8-ASEAN-Declaration-on-Digital-Tourism_FINAL.pdf.

Data and Methodology

To obtain a measurable, comparable, and readily replicable benchmark of a country's capability to activate the process of smart tourism, the study has identified relevant indicators. These are derived from the subprinciples of smart tourism, broken down into parameters and subparameters (Table 5). Data sources for these indicators include the World Economic Forum's Tourism and Travel Development Index, the World Bank's World Development Indicators, and UNWTO's Tourism Data Dashboard. For some of the indicators, the study team referred to other public sources.

The availability of indicators used to measure the subpillars varies across the relevant period, which ends in the first quarter of 2023. For example, international tourist arrivals data are available only until 2019 for all the countries; however, data points such as Internet quality can be tracked in real time, and thus the latest values of such indicators are considered. The range of values of indicators varies as well. For instance, indicators taken from the Travel and Tourism Development Index 2021 include survey-based indicators whose value varies from 0 to 7, with 7 representing the best scenario. Meanwhile, indicators such as the "Official tourist app" take binary values and others are reported as percentages. Additionally, some of the indicators used are not directly comparable across countries. For example, the indicator "vegetal forest" cover will logically have lower values in countries with less land area.

To overcome these challenges, indicators are first normalized using appropriate procedures, such as dividing the vegetal forest cover by a country's land area. Second, the normalized values are converted to uniform scale using the following formula:

$$X_{final} = 100 * \frac{X - X_{min}}{X_{max} - X_{min}}$$

This formula converts all the initial values in the range of 0–100 and provides a clear idea of how a country is performing on a given indicator compared to the worst- and best-performing countries in the group. To calculate the final score for the parameter under consideration, the average score of respective subparameters is considered. The scores at the parameter level are then aggregated to obtain the performance level at the subprinciple level. These in turn are combined to arrive at a value for performance at the principle level.

Table 5: **Framework for Assessing Country-Level Readiness for Smart Tourism**

Principle	Subprinciple	Parameter	Subparameter	Source	Year
Attractiveness	Smart attraction	Digital visiting	Official tourist app	Study Team Research	2023
		City attractiveness	Smart city projects	ASEAN Smart Cities Network: Monitoring and Evaluation Report 2022	2022
		Cost of staying in country	Hotel price index	WEF TTDI Dashboard	2021
			Purchasing power parity	World Bank: World Development Indicators	2021
		Destination attractiveness	Number of world heritage sites	UNESCO World Heritage List Statistics	2023
			International inbound tourists	UNWTO Tourism Data Dashboard	2019
			International tourism expenditure	UNWTO Tourism Data Dashboard	2019
		Availability of hotels	Hotel infrastructure in terms of number of hotels and rooms	UNWTO Tourism Data Dashboard	2020
	Smart amenities	Tech-enabled experience	Free public Wi-Fi	Wi-Fi Map	2023
			Free hotel Wi-Fi	Booking.com	2023
		E-commerce and ticketing	Online merchant payments	World Bank: The Global Findex Database 2021	2021
			UNCTAD B2C E-commerce Index	UNCTAD B2C E-Commerce Index 2020	2020
		Others	Car rental facilities	WEF TTDI Dashboard	2021
			Number of ATMs	World Bank: World Development Indicators	2021
	Smart content	Visibility of country's tourism board online	Country branding strategy	WEF TTDI Dashboard	2021
			Interactivity on tourism website	Study Team Research	2023
	Online popularity	Digital demand	Digital demand for natural tourism	WEF TTDI Dashboard	2021
			Digital demand for cultural and entertainment tourism	WEF TTDI Dashboard	2021
		Social media presence	Presence on Instagram (Number of followers and posts)	Instagram	2023
			Presence on Twitter (Number of followers)	Twitter	2023

continued on next page

Table 5 *continued*

Principle	Subprinciple	Parameter	Subparameter	Source	Year
Accessibility	Smart mobility	Ease of travelling to country	Visa friendliness	Passport index: Welcoming Countries Rank 2023	2023
		Availability and quality of modes of transport	Air transport infrastructure	WEF TTDI Dashboard	2021
			Ground transport infrastructure	WEF TTDI Dashboard	2021
		Smartness of mobility in smart cities	Car sharing apps	International Institute for Management Development Smart Cities Index Report 2023	2023
			Smart parking		
			Bicycle hiring		
			Online ticket sales		
			Information availability		
	Smart convenience	Ease of payments	Electronic payments	World Bank: The Global Findex Database 2021	2021
		Ease of availing services	3G mobile network coverage	ITU Digital Development Dashboard	2021
			4G mobile network coverage		
			Internet quality (Average mobile and broadband download speed)	Speed test by Ookla	2023
			Digital identities	Global Data Regulation Diagnostic Survey Dataset 2021	2021
			Security of digital identity	International Civil Aviation Organization Public Key Directory Participants	2023
			Use of digital platform for providing financial services	WEF TTDI Dashboard	2021
			Use of digital platforms for providing transportation and shipping		
			Use of digital platforms for providing hotels, restaurants, and leisure activities services		
	Barrier-free designs	Inclusivity in the country	Economic inequality	World Economics: Gini coefficient	2021
			Gender inequality	WEF Global Gender Gap Report 2020	2020
			Disability friendly	Booking.com	2023

continued on next page

Table 5 *continued*

Principle	Subprinciple	Parameter	Subparameter	Source	Year
Sustainability	Life and tourism environment	Environmental sustainability	CO_2 emissions	Our World in Data: Per capita CO_2 emissions	2021
			Water stress	World Bank: World Development Indicators	2020
			Air quality	IQAir: World's most polluted countries and regions	2022
			Vegetal forest cover	World Bank: World Development Indicators	2020
			Protected areas	Protected Planet: Protected areas and OECMs	2021
		Digital skills gap	Digital skills institutions	Wiley Digital Skills Gap Index 2021	2021
			Digital responsiveness		
			Government support		
			Supply, demand, and competitiveness		
			Data ethics and integrity		
			Academia research intensity		
	City resilience	Business resilience	Economic factors	FM Global Resilience Index 2022	2022
			Risk quality factors		
			Supply chain factors		
		Cybersecurity	Cybersecurity risks	ITU Global Cybersecurity Index 2020	2020
		Population	Population density	World Bank: World Development Indicators	2021
	Creativity and innovation	Start-up environment	Quantity of start-ups	Start-up Blink Global Star-up Ecosystem Index 2022	2022
			Quality of start-ups		
			Business environment		
		Creative output	Intangible assets	WIPO Global Innovation Index 2022	2022
			Creative goods and services		
			Online creativity		
		City environment	Creative cities	UNESCO Creative Cities	2023
	Tourism safety	Safety and security	Business cost of crime and violence	WEF TTDI Dashboard	2021
			Reliability of police services		
			Safety walking alone at night		
			Homicide rate		
			Global terrorism index		
			Organized violence, deaths		

continued on next page

Table 5 *continued*

Principle	Subprinciple	Parameter	Subparameter	Source	Year
		Health and hygiene	Physician density		
			Use of basic sanitation		
			Use of basic drinking water		
			Hospital beds intensity		
			Accessibility of healthcare services		
			Communicable disease incidence		
Collaborative Partnerships	Smart governance	E-government online services	Institutional framework	UN E-Government Survey 2022	2022
			Content provision		
			Services provision		
			E-participation		
			Technology		
		Open government information	Open data inventory score	Open Data Watch: Open Data Inventory	2022
		Prioritization of travel and tourism industry	Travel and tourism government expenditure	WEF TTDI Dashboard	2021
			Comprehensiveness of travel and tourism data		
			Timeliness of travel and tourism data		
			Travel and tourism capital investment		
	Public–Private collaboration	Public–private partnerships	Country's adherence to the best regulatory practices	World Bank: PPPs Regulatory Quality	2018
			Investment value per PPP project	World Bank: Benchmarking Infrastructure Development	2014–2018

ASEAN = Association of Southeast Asian Nations; ATM = automated teller machine; B2C = business-to-consumer; CO_2 = carbon dioxide; ITU = International Telecommunication Union; OECM = other effective area-based conservation measure; PPP = public–private partnership; TTDI = Travel and Tourism Development Index; UNCTAD = United Nations Conference on Trade and Development; UNESCO = United Nations Educational, Scientific and Cultural Organization; UNWTO = United Nations World Tourism Organization; WEF = World Economic Forum; WIPO = World Intellectual Property Organization.

Note: Where data is unavailable for a few countries for some indicators for the given year, the latest available data point for that country is considered.

Source: Authors.

Evaluation of Readiness of ASEAN Countries

Figure 18 illustrates results of the framework and shows final scores for 6 of the 10 ASEAN countries where data for all indicators were available. Singapore clearly scores highest on most parameters (18 of 31), making it a clear leader on smart tourism. A similar analysis is also performed at an aggregate level to rank individual principles and is illustrated in subsequent chapters.

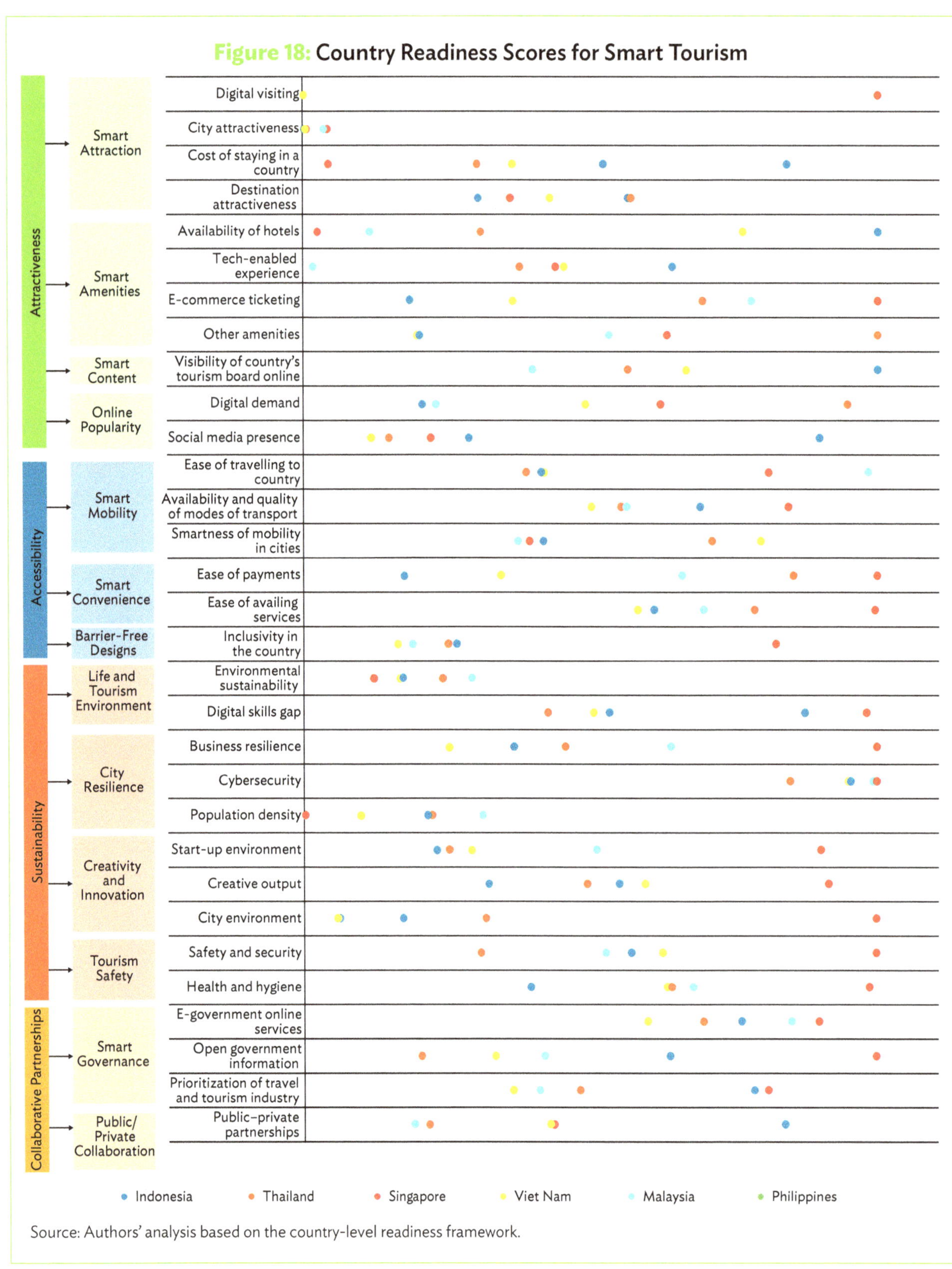

Figure 18: Country Readiness Scores for Smart Tourism

Source: Authors' analysis based on the country-level readiness framework.

Principle 1: Attractiveness

Figure 19 shows that Indonesia leads the way on the "attractiveness" principle, with an overall average score of 60, followed by Thailand, Singapore, and the Philippines. Malaysia, the Philippines, and Thailand score highest on smart attraction because of their interactive and illustrative official tourist apps that allow tourists independence and self-reliance in a new country. Thailand leads ASEAN member countries in smart amenities by enabling e-commerce, online ticketing, and other tourism-related services, especially car rental facilities and density of automated teller machines.

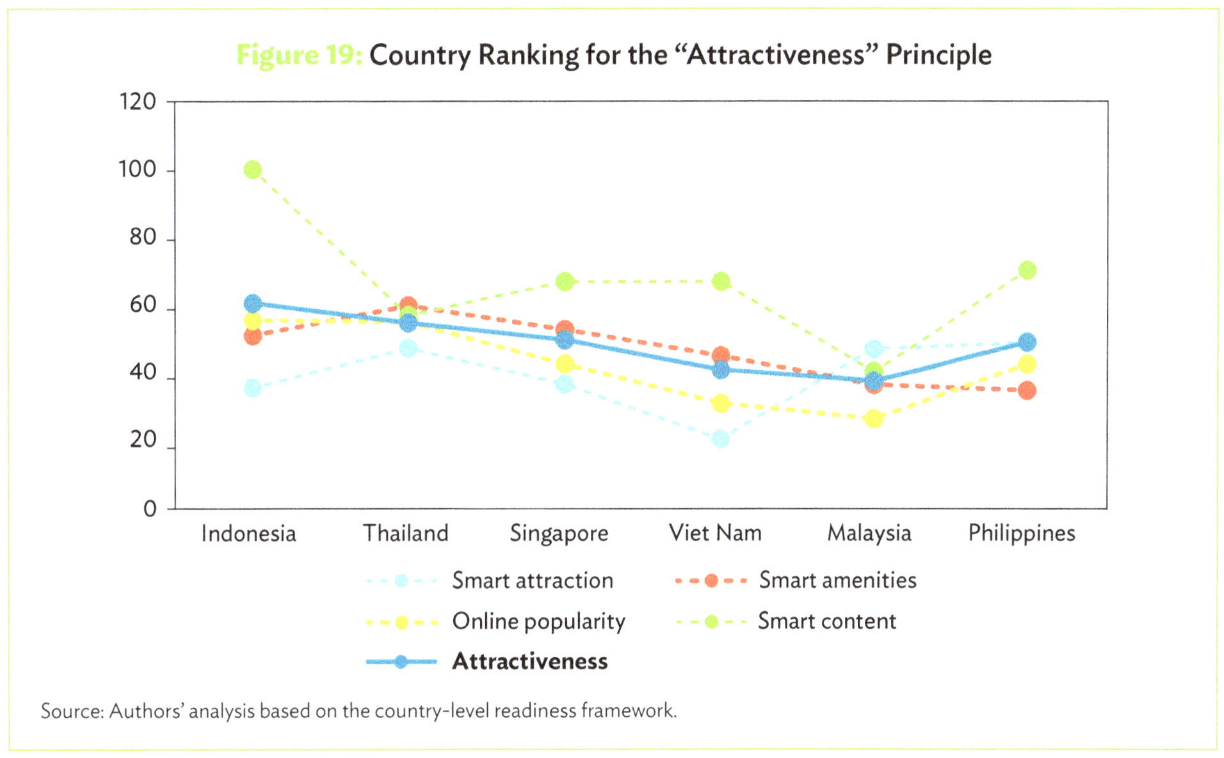

Figure 19: Country Ranking for the "Attractiveness" Principle

Source: Authors' analysis based on the country-level readiness framework.

Indonesia's efforts in smart content have been noteworthy and have been benchmarked with an outstanding country branding strategy rating by the National Tourism Organization. However, Thailand has gained maximum digital demand, measured by the aggregate online search volume on brandtags of natural, cultural, and entertainment tourism.

Principle 2: Accessibility

Figure 20 shows that Singapore is by far best among ASEAN countries on accessibility, scoring highest on each of the subprinciples, followed by Thailand, Malaysia, and Viet Nam. Singapore and Malaysia lead on the smart mobility pillar owing to "better transport infrastructure" for Singapore and "visa-friendly policies" for Malaysia. While Viet Nam and Thailand provide the best services in smart mobility services in the cities, they fall behind on providing air transport infrastructure and ground transport infrastructure.

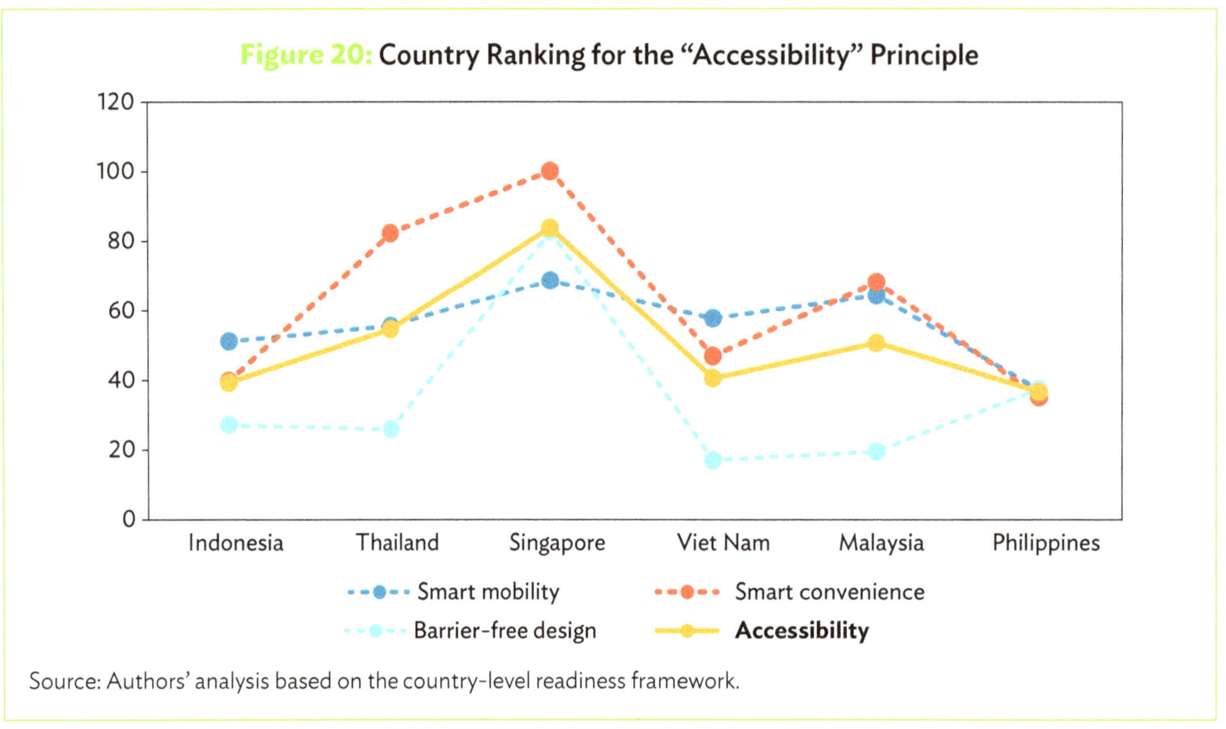

Figure 20: Country Ranking for the "Accessibility" Principle

Source: Authors' analysis based on the country-level readiness framework.

Singapore's robust Internet economy, use of digital identities, digital platforms, and digital payments earn it the first position on "smart convenience," followed by Thailand and Malaysia.

On "barrier-free designs," Singapore's efforts such as "wheelchair-accessible mass rapid transit system,"[13] and higher number of hotels providing disabled-friendly services make it the most barrier-free country in the region.

Principle 3: Sustainability

Figure 21 shows that Singapore again leads this principle, as well scoring highest on three of the four subprinciples, followed by Malaysia, Viet Nam, and Thailand. Malaysia and Singapore have a robust digital skills ecosystem, enabling them to score higher on "life and tourism environmentt" despite scoring low on environmental sustainability. However, the efforts of Singapore, such as the sustainable Gardens by the Bay, are noteworthy.[14] Even in city resilience, Singapore and Malaysia are the best-performing ASEAN countries, with both having resilient business environments and cybersecurity measures. For example, Singapore's tourism board has its own personal data protection policy safeguarding tourists' personal information.[15]

---

[13]   *Medical Assistance4u*. 2022. Transportation Options for People with Mobility Issues. 1 August. https://medicalassistance4u.care/transportation-options-for-people-with-mobility-issues/.

[14]   Gardens by the Bay. https://www.gardensbythebay.com.sg/.

[15]   Singapore Tourism Board. Personal Data Protection Policy. https://www.visitsingapore.com/madewithpassion/privacy/.

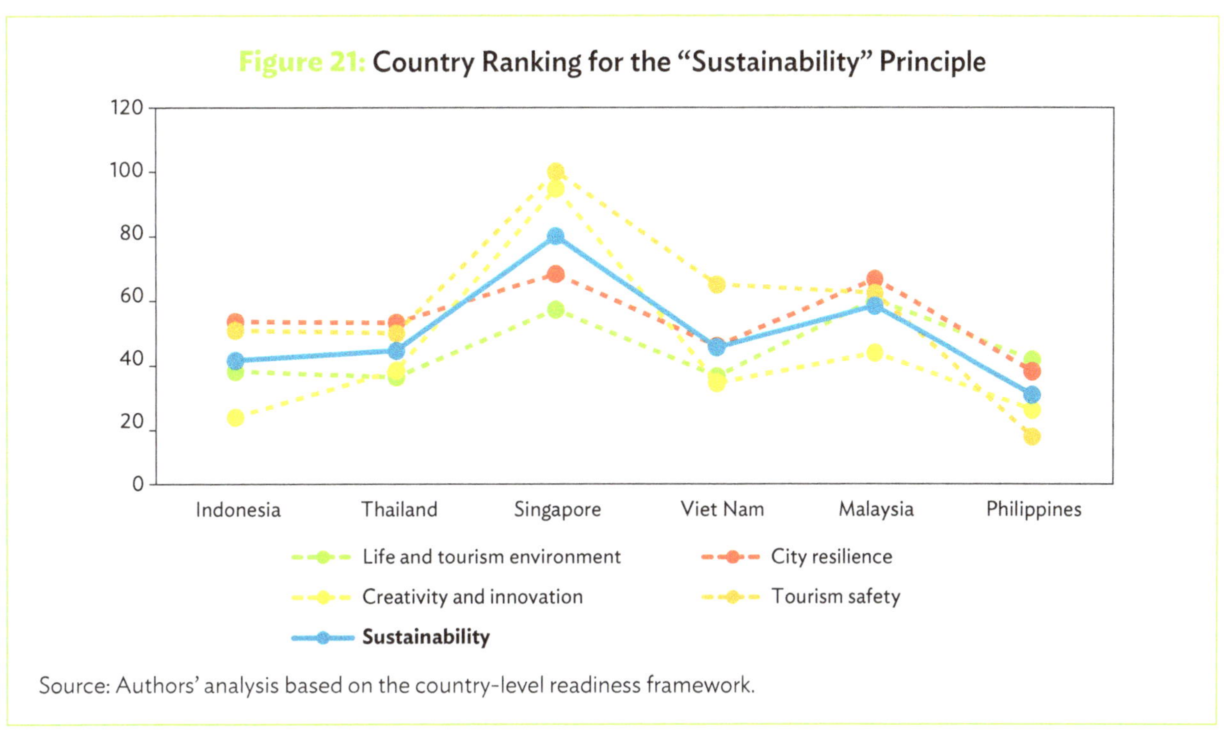

Source: Authors' analysis based on the country-level readiness framework.

Singapore's efforts for the start-up ecosystem, such as the establishment of the Start-up SG[16] platform helps relevant firms connect with relevant stakeholders. Singapore also leads in creative output with the highest score for "creative industry" and "online creativity." This has helped Singapore achieve top spot under the creativity and innovation subprinciple. For tourism safety, Singapore again scores highest on "safety and security" and "health and hygiene." Contactless travel at Singapore airports offers FAST (Fast and Seamless Travel) service for departing passengers, allowing them to complete check-in, baggage drop, immigration, and boarding without human intervention.[17]

Principle 4: Collaborative Partnerships

Figure 22 shows that for the "collaborative partnerships" principle, Indonesia leads among ASEAN member countries. The government's committed efforts to provide a holistic and flawless experience to citizens and tourists have yielded favorable outcomes. There is strict adherence to regulatory practices by parties in PPP projects as well as a high investment value per PPP project in Indonesia. However, Singapore benchmarks smart governance. For instance, the Tourism Information and Service Hub and the Singapore Tourism Analytics Network provide tourists and citizens with information and insights on events, entertainment, and travel services in the country.

---

[16]   StartupSG. https://www.startupsg.gov.sg/.
[17]   Changi Airport Group. Fast and Seamless Travel. https://www.changiairport.com/en/airport-guide/departing/checking-in/fast-check-in.html.

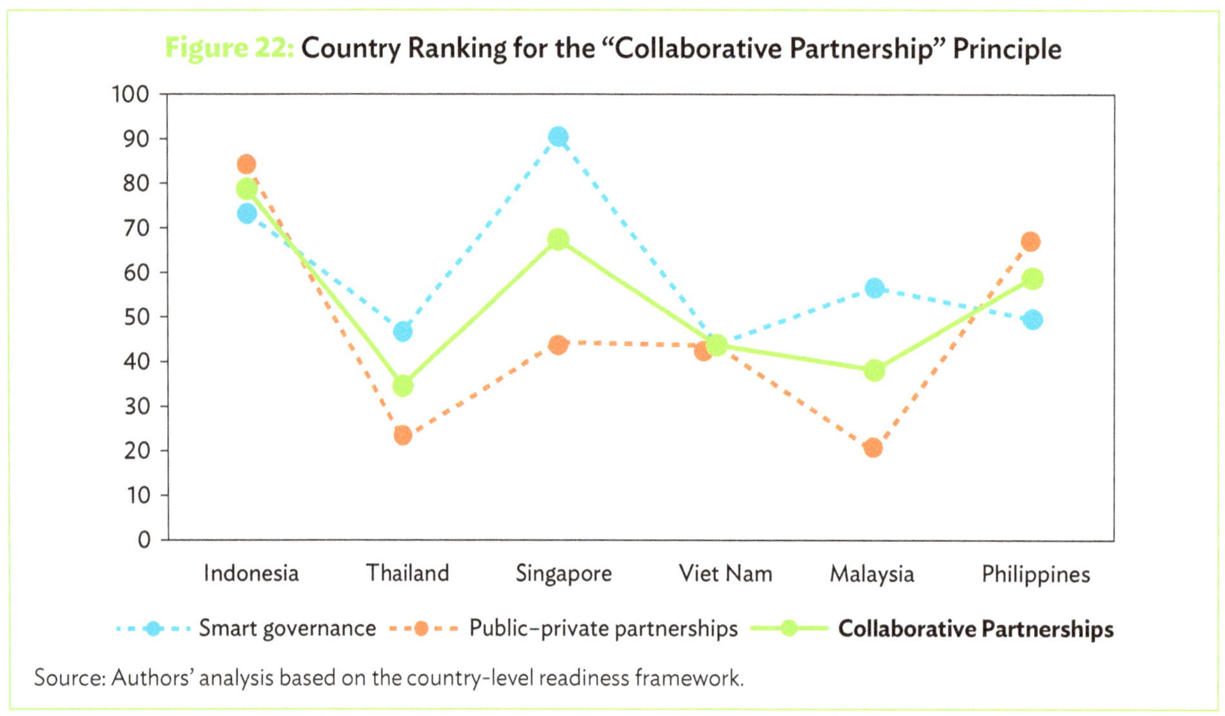

Figure 22: Country Ranking for the "Collaborative Partnership" Principle

Source: Authors' analysis based on the country-level readiness framework.

Conclusion

Clearly, countries often differ on level of development on smart tourism. Their varying resources affect their capacities to leverage and benefit from digitalization tools. The situation gets more challenging for the large proportion of SMEs present in the tourism sector, as well as with seasonal fluctuations in productivity and high casual and seasonal labor (Dredge et al. 2019). This implies that the transition from e-tourism to smart tourism will not happen at the same pace for all countries. Development of regional policies for smart tourism needs to consider the stages of digital development of constituent countries. Policies and programs at national and regional levels become important to narrow the digital divide so that over time a region-wide smart tourism can be developed for better and resilient economic prospects.

Many regional organizations, like ASEAN and Central Asia Regional Economic Cooperation (CAREC), aspire to form a smart tourism destination among their constituent countries. This implies that, in addition to marketing countries as single tourist destination, they need to expand the discussion of digital economy beyond their national boundaries. They need to bring countries together to commit to coherent policies and regional digital agreements. Some countries have started moving in this direction. While some aspect of digital economy has already been discussed in trade agreements, such as Regional Comprehensive Economic Partnership (RCEP) and the Comprehensive and Progressive Agreement for Trans-Pacific Partnership (CPTPP), more recently countries have adopted a more comprehensive approach—i.e., the Digital Economy Partnership Agreement (DEPA) and the Australia–Singapore Digital Economy Agreement (ASDEA)—to enable sectors to undergo digital transformation. This assumes importance for the tourism sector as countries decide to transition from e-tourism to smart tourism. The next chapter looks into selected regional cooperation initiatives to understand their status and gaps in policies in cross-border digital economy.

4 Examining Digital Economy Agreements for Regional Smart Tourism

This chapter looks into the third strand of the study framework—issues of digitalization—to reveal ways to maximize the potential from participation in a digitalized economy. The issues of digitalization as presented in Chapter 1 stem from a framework proposed in 2021 by the Pacific Economic Cooperation Council (PECC). They are important for advancing a country's stage of digitalization from basic, to intermediate, and through advanced, and its position in the smart tourism ecosystem. The chapter looks at selected regional agreements where countries have decided to work with each other for undertaking digital reforms in a coherent fashion across national boundaries. Sectors undergoing such coherent transformation can offer greater economies of scale and, hence, bigger economic benefits.

Regional Cooperation in Digital Economy Expands Market for Smart Tourism

Provisions of the digital economy enable smart tourism. So far, the digital economy has been driven by the rapid expansion of the Internet, which in turn is underpinned by the development of information technology and informatization. The digital economy gives rise to two issues: (i) infrastructure,which covers communications and Internet technologies; and (ii) digital activities that cover platforms, digital solutions, digital content, and e-commerce (Li 2017). Meanwhile, recent studies have established a positive and robust relationship between the digital economy and the tourism sector (Zhao, Mei, and Xiao 2022).

However, digitalization has created a new set of policy considerations. Increasing digitalization has given rise to concerns about data sharing, regulatory gaps, cross-border data flows, interoperability of digital identity, and use of personal data. The traditional industry-specific policymaking approach does not cater to the cross-sector nature of digital economy and, thus, fails to meet expected economic growth and social development outcomes (PECC 2021). The PECC's report on digital economy highlights issues faced by the digital ecosystem (PECC 2021). It has classified these issues into three categories of *digital economy* (focusing on the domestic digital policies of cybersecurity, privacy, competition policy, and others); *digital trade* (focusing on regional and global cooperation on data flow, standardization, data protection, regulatory coherence, and others); and *crosscutting issues* (digital and development, digital and small business, digital divide, and others) (Figure 23).

Figure 23: Overview of Key Digital Economy and Digital Trade Issues

Digital Economy Issues

Foundational Policy Issues

1. Data Protection and Privacy
As economies and businesses digitalize, keeping user data secure and private is paramount to building consumer and investor trust.

2. Cybersecurity
Cybersecurity has a significant impact on digital trust, and often intersects with questions on data protection, as well as implication for critical infrastructure.

3. Competition Policy
Digital players creating extensive ecosystems of complementary products and services disrupt the status quo, exposing regulatory gaps.

4. Consumer Protection
Concerns arising when digital platforms track, monitor, and profile users without their knowledge or consent across centralized and decentralized platforms.

5. Intellectual Property
The digital economy allows creators to disseminate content faster and wider than ever, but IP rules tend to be too strong in some areas, discouraging innovation, and too weak in others, disadvantaging creators.

Application Issues

1. Digital Identity
Interoperable digital ID systems keep data secure and portable, enabling verification and authentication for in person, online, and remote services.

2. Data Sharing
Standardizing data exchange protocols fosters innovation, economic integration, and dynamism by facilitating interoperability across systems and jurisdictions.

3. Quality of Service
Spikes in data traffic volumes can result in operators facing difficulties in their QoS requirements –amplified due to COVID-19

Emerging Issues

1. Artificial Intelligence
The lack of transparency surrounding AI algorithms is a growing issue, especially when they are put in charge of life-altering decisions

2. Intermediate Liability
As digital platforms grow, they unwittingly turn into disseminators and amplifiers of potentially harmful content, raising question on ownership and responsibility.

3. Content Moderation
Content moderation can be a predominant issue in certain jurisdictions when rules are unclear about what is considered prohibited content and who it applies to.

Digital Trade Issues

Core Issues

1. Cross-Border Data Flows
Enhanced connectivity increases data generation, storage, access, and exchange, both locally and globally. Constraints within the system create friction and hinder digital trade.

2. Data Sovereignty
Data sovereignty means that the economies where data is collected or processed have the authority to access, regulate, and impact that data based on their laws and regulations.

Process Enablers

1. Data Transfer Mechanisms
Data transfer mechanisms bridge data protection differences, using certifications and agreements instead of revising laws.

2. Digital Trade Standards
Digital trade standards enable interoperability across systems, processes, and technologies, increasing the security, safety, quality, and reliability of goods and services.

Emerging Issues

1. Regulatory Fragmentation
Economies are at different stages of creating, implementing, or enforcing digital trade regulations, creating barriers for cross-border business and inhibiting trade opportunities.

2. Digital Regulatory Arbitrage
Global companies registering multiple subsidiaries digitally in different jurisdictions can evade domestic regulations by structuring their transactions to take advantage of foreign regulatory regimes.

Crosscutting

1. Digital and Development
Although the extent of digitalization is different in low-income and high-income economies, countries can take advantage of innovative data use of digital technologies that are available.

2. Driving Inclusivity and Closing the Digital Divide
Inclusivity involves bridging the digital divide by providing equal access to digital technologies, promoting digital literacy, and ensuring affordability.

3. Digitalization of Big and Small Businesses
Digitalization benefits both big and small businesses, offering them increased efficiency, streamlined processes, and access to a wider market.

4. Green Digitalization and Sustainability
Digitalization enables environmentally sustainable growth through various means, including monitoring energy usage in smart buildings, adopting electric or hydrogen-fueled vehicles, etc.

AI = artificial intelligence, COVID-19 = coronavirus disease, IP = intellectual property, QOS = quality of service.

Source: Pacific Economic Cooperation Council. 2021. *Primer on Economic Integration Issues Posed by the Digital Economy*. Singapore.

Often, a critical issue in digitalization is how far countries should advance the relevant public policies beyond their national boundaries and advance their existing regional cooperation measures in the tourism sector. Regional cooperation allows governments and stakeholders to coordinate policies, share costs of building and maintaining infrastructure, and expand markets to advance the digital economy. Regional cooperation initiatives also help build trust crucial for digital development among countries. In addition, digital advancement promotes regional cooperation in trade, finance, transport, energy, and other sectors (Tang and Cortez 2023). The report, Digital Societies in Asia Pacific: Progressing towards Digital Nations, shows how fast countries progress toward full-fledged digital societies depends on the level of collaboration across government, the private sector, and other nonstate institutions (Okeleke and Joiner 2022).

However, data localization is a major contentious issue in digital economy cooperation. Digital sovereignty is often associated with the need to store data within national borders, but the link between the geographic storage of data and development is not evident. However, discussion about cross-border data flows has remained a challenge for policymakers; consensus is growing that data flow across borders is necessary for equitable distribution of benefits, within and across countries, provided risks related to privacy and national security are addressed (UNCTAD 2021). This is particularly important for the tourism sector as it benefits from digital transformation both within and across countries. Related to digitalization, tourism stands to benefit on the high amount of data involved in tourist flows and business transactions (Tussyadiah, Li, and Miller 2019). Data and the analytics generated from the same (known as big data) are said to improve policymaking and business operation for sustainable tourism in the future. Thus, literature has offered a conceptual framework for ethical data management and data governance in the tourism and hospitality sector (Yallop et al. 2021). This framework would enable careful consideration of ethical and security considerations in the collection, storage, and analysis of tourism and hospitality data and information, in the best interests of stakeholders involved. It can be argued that the framework will be more effective if crafted and implemented at the regional level.

Review of Cooperation Initiatives to Promote a Digital Ecosystem

Existing regional cooperation initiatives have creators.ed frameworks for enabling digitalization at a regional level. Organizations such as ASEAN, the Asia-Pacific Economic Cooperation (APEC), and CAREC have forged agreements reflecting their willingness to cooperate on digital economy to promote trade, investment, and industrial competitiveness. APEC members have charted the APEC Internet and Digital Economy Roadmap[18] and have agreed to identify and secure critical information infrastructure,[19] while implementing the Cross-Border Privacy Rules System.[20]

Meanwhile, ASEAN has acknowledged the 4th Industrial Revolution through a consolidated strategy[21] and is working on bridging the gap in digital connectivity among its members.[22] To realize digital trade potential, the ASEAN Digital Masterplan 2025 is in place, backed by the ASEAN Data Management Framework, the ASEAN Framework on Personal Data Protection, and the ASEAN Model Contractual Clauses for Cross-Border Data Flows.[23]

CAREC has also undertaken several initiatives to focus on digital economy, some of which are highlighted in Box 2.

---

[18]   The APEC Internet and Digital Economy Roadmap guides technological and policy exchanges among member economies; promotes innovative, inclusive, and savailable. growth; and bridges the digital divide in the APEC region. APEC Viet Nam. 2017. *APEC Internet and Digital Economy Roadmap*. Paper prepared for the Concluding Senior Officials' Meeting. Da Nang, Viet Nam. 6-7 November. http://mddb.apec.org/Documents/2017/SOM/CSOM/17_csom_006.pdf.

[19]   Critical information infrastructure should be understood as referring to interconnected information systems and networks, the disruption or destruction of which would have serious impact on the health, safety, security, or economic well-being of citizens, or on the effective functioning of government or the economy. See definition in OECD. 2008. *OECD Recommendation of the Council on the Protection of Critical Information Infrastructures*. Paper presented at the OECD Ministerial Meeting on the Future of the Internet Economy. Seoul, 17–18 June. https://www.oecd.org/sti/40825404.pdf.

[20]   The APEC Cross-Border Privacy Rules system is a government-backed data privacy certification that companies can join to demonstrate compliance with internationally recognized data privacy protections. For more information, see the factsheet at APEC. 2023. What is the Cross-Border Privacy Rules System? https://www.apec.org/about-us/about-apec/fact-sheets/what-is-the-cross-border-privacy-rules-system.

[21]   The Consolidated Strategy on the Fourth Industrial Revolution for ASEAN aims to provide policy guidance in building the ASEAN Digital Economy across three pillars of ASEAN: the ASEAN Political-Security Community, the ASEAN Economic Community, and the ASEAN Socio-Cultural Community. ASEAN. 2021. *Consolidated Strategy on the Fourth Industrial Revolution for ASEAN*. Jakarta: ASEAN Secretariat. http://aadcp2.org/wp-content/uploads/6.-Consolidated-Strategy-on-the-4IR-for-ASEAN.pdf.

[22]   The Masterplan on ASEAN Connectivity 2025 envisions a seamlessly and comprehensively connected and integrated ASEAN to promote competitiveness, inclusiveness, and a greater sense of community. ASEAN. 2017. *Master Plan on ASEAN Connectivity 2025*. Jakarta: ASEAN Secretariat. https://asean.org/wp-content/uploads/2018/01/47.-December-2017-MPAC2025-2nd-Reprint-.pdf.

[23]   The ASEAN Data Management Framework provides guidelines for businesses of data management frameworks; the ASEAN Framework on Personal Data Protection aims to strengthen the protection of personal data in the region; and the ASEAN Model Contractual Clauses for Cross-Border Data Flows provides model clauses, which could be used in legal-binding agreements between two parties

Box 2: CAREC's Initiatives to Promote Digital Economy

The Central Asia Regional Economic Cooperation's (CAREC) Integrated Trade Agenda 2030 and Rolling Strategic Action Plan 2018–2020 aim to strengthen CAREC's trade expansion and economic diversification by focusing on trade expansion from increased market access, greater diversification, and stronger institutions for trade.

One of the Integrated Trade Agenda's interventions includes promotion of digital trade through knowledge sharing of best practices and frameworks on e-commerce. The objective of Customs Cooperation Committee under the agenda also includes promoting innovation on digital trade initiatives, such as customs technology, supply chain management, and paperless trade. The Rolling Strategic Action Plan also lists initiatives or projects related to digital economy.

Initiative	Description	Relevant Issues
Information common exchange	Customs data exchange among member countries linked to the CAREC Advanced Transit System Pilot	Data sharing
Paperless trading or e-certification of trade documents	Promoting best practices on paperless trade with potential interconnectivity and interoperability via electronic data exchange or regional single window	Paperless trading
Developing trade in services	Study to promote expansion and integration of trade in services in priority areas (tourism, finance, health, pharmaceutical, etc.)	Data sharing
Promotion of e-commerce and innovation (Industry 4.0)	Scoping study for the adoption of e-commerce and other technologies like blockchain, Internet of Things, big data in trade Pilot initiative on World Customs Organization framework of standards in cross-border e-commerce Seminar on best practices or field visits to promote digital trade	Digital development Quality of service Data sharing

Apart from these initiatives, other strategy documents like the CAREC Digital Strategy 2030[a] also focus on various pillars of digital economy: leadership, governance, and investment in digital economy; digital policy enablers and safeguards; digital infrastructure, resilience, and platforms; digital skills and competencies; and innovation, entrepreneurship, and information and communication technology competitiveness.

[a] CAREC Digital Strategy 2030 aims to create a data-driven digital regional economy with fast and reliable online access to relevant information and trusted, real-time, user-friendly digital services for all citizens, businesses, and administrations across the CAREC region, see https://www.adb.org/sites/default/files/institutional-document/777876/carec-digital-strategy-2030.pdf.

Sources: Asian Development Bank (ADB). 2019. *CAREC Integrated Trade Agenda 2030 and Rolling Strategic Action Plan 2018–2020.* Manila; and ADB. 2022. *CAREC Digital Strategy 2030: Accelerating Digital Transformation for Regional Competitiveness and Inclusive Growth. Manila.*

Despite ongoing discussions about the digital economy, these regions are yet to comprehensively address digital economy issues. For example, Figure 24 shows that on the Digital Trade Restrictiveness Index, which includes a cross-country compilation of policy measures that can restrict digital trade, Asia and the Pacific remains the most restrictive region (UNOHRLLS and WTO 2022).

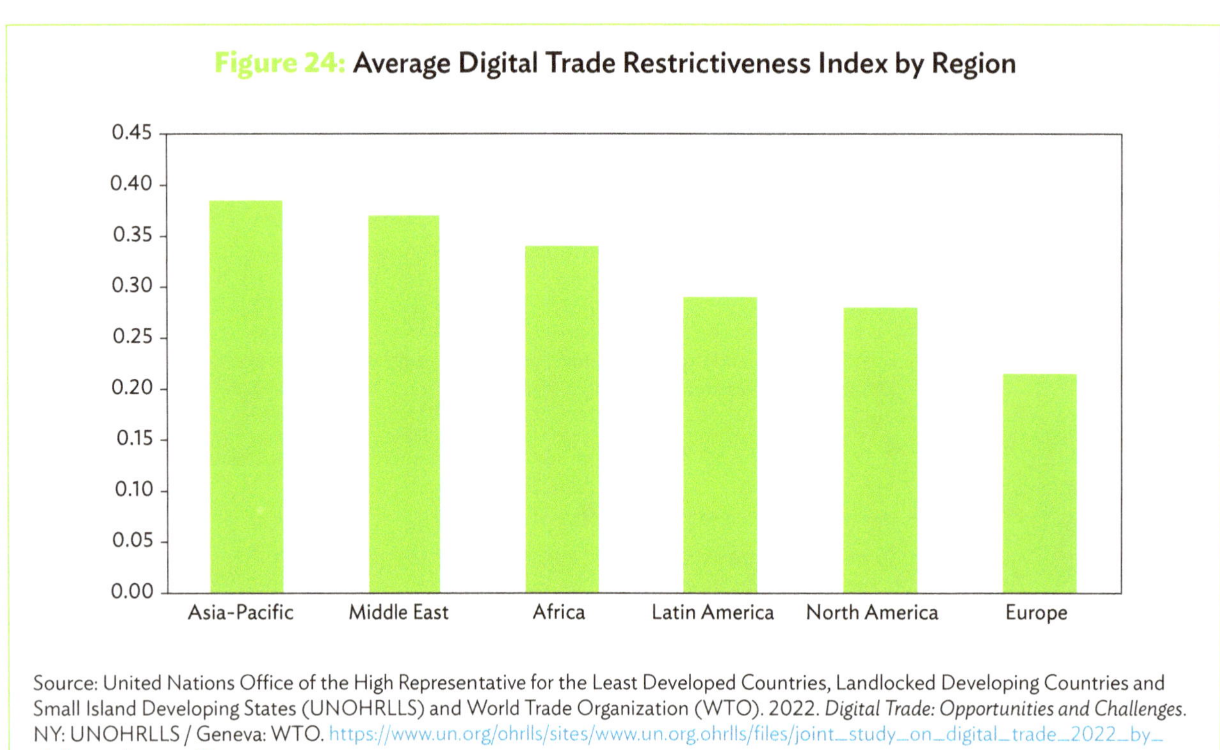

Figure 24: Average Digital Trade Restrictiveness Index by Region

Source: United Nations Office of the High Representative for the Least Developed Countries, Landlocked Developing Countries and Small Island Developing States (UNOHRLLS) and World Trade Organization (WTO). 2022. *Digital Trade: Opportunities and Challenges.* NY: UNOHRLLS / Geneva: WTO. https://www.un.org/ohrlls/sites/www.un.org.ohrlls/files/joint_study_on_digital_trade_2022_by_ohrlls_and_wto.pdf.

New agreements are trying to comprehensively address digital economy cooperation. These include the digital economy agreements and the Digital Economy Partnership Agreement (DEPA) among Singapore, Chile, and New Zealand.[24] These agreements are "digital only agreements" that establish digital trade rules and digital economy collaborations between two or more economies. Through such agreements, governments come together to set guidelines and collaborate on data infrastructure to address digital policy fragmentation. Such cooperation and targeted policy discussion helps all sectors to accelerate the digital economy, including trade and tourism.[25]

This chapter compares four of the most recent agreements across various issues as outlined in the PECC Primer: the Australia-Singapore Digital Economy Agreement (ASDEA), DEPA, the Comprehensive and Progressive Agreement for Trans-Pacific Partnership (CPTPP), and the Regional Comprehensive Economic Partnership (RCEP). Although CPTPP and RCEP are not "digital only agreements", they incorporate a chapter on electronic commerce which covers issues related to the digital ecosystem.

---

[24] At present, four such agreements are in place: DEPA, the United Kingdom–Singapore Digital Economy Agreement, the [Republic of] Korea–Singapore Digital Economy Agreement, and ASDEA.

[25] United Nations. 2022. *Digital Trade Agreements and E-commerce in FTA: The ASEAN and Pacific Experiences.* Presentation for the Capacity Building Workshop – Navigating Digital Trade Law Landscape. Part 2: Country Experiences. Bangkok. 14 December. https://www.unescap.org/sites/default/d8files/event-documents/Sven_UNESCAP%20UNCITRAL.pdf.

The analysis follows a method similar to the one used in the World Economic Forum's "Advancing Digital Trade in Asia" report (WEF 2020). The most common topics related to the digital economy have been collated and mapped to the relevant issues from the PECC primer. The comprehensiveness of the discussion has been evaluated based on the number of subtopics covered in each chapter. For example, topics on personal information protection include recognizing benefits of data protection, establishing legal frameworks, defining key principles, and the mention of trust-marks or certifications. ASDEA and DEPA cover nearly all these topics, whereas the CPTPP and the RCEP cover only a few.

The comparison matrix (Table 6) is a comprehensive analysis of how regional groupings are addressing various topics related to the digital economy and digital trade. Of the four agreements taken, ASDEA and DEPA are more exhaustive on digital issues compared with the CPTPP and the RCEP. ASDEA touches on nearly all the issues, closely followed by DEPA. The CPTPP and the RCEP do not address important aspects such as digital identity, open government data, and artificial intelligence. This could be primarily because of the bilateral nature of ASDEA that provides an opportunity to go into greater depth. The next chapter provides policy recommendations for enabling regional cooperation across relatively less addressed issues in the digital agreements.

Table 6: Comparison of Digital Provisions in Regional Agreements

Issue	Relevant Chapters	ASDEA	DEPA	CPTPP	RCEP
Digital Economy					
Data protection and privacy	Personal information protection	✓ +	✓ +	✓ –	✓ –
	Cryptography	✓	✓	✗	✗
Cybersecurity	Cybersecurity	✓ +	✓ +	✓ –	✓ –
Competition policy	Nondiscrimination of digital products	✓	✓	✓	✗
	Cooperation on competition policy[a]	✓ +	✓ +	✓ –	✓ –
Intellectual property	Source code	✓ +	✗	✓ –	✗
	Intellectual property	✗	✓ –	✓ +	✓ +
Consumer protection	Online consumer protection	✓ +	✓ +	✓ –	✓ –
	Spam (Unsolicited messages)	✓	✓	✓	✓
	Safe online environment	✓ +	✓ –	✗	✗
Digital identity	Digital identity	✓	✓	✗	✗
	Electronic signature/authentication	✓	✗	✓	✓
Data sharing	Open government data	✓	✓	✗	✗
Quality of service	Standards and conformity assessment	✓	✗	✗	✗
	Dispute settlement[a]	✓	✓	✓	✓
Artificial intelligence	AI or emerging technologies	✓	✓	✗	✗

continued on next page

Table 6 *continued*

Issue	Relevant Chapters	ASDEA	DEPA	CPTPP	RCEP
Digital Trade					
Cross-border data flows	Allowing data flow	✓ +	✓ +	✓ +	✓ −
	Data localization	✓	✓	✓	✓
	Data localization for financial services	✓	✗	✗	✗
	Custom duties	✓ −	✓ −	✓ −	✓ +
Data transfer mechanisms	Domestic e-transaction framework	✓ +	✓ +	✓ −	✓ −
Digital trade standards	E-invoicing	✓	✓	✗	✗
	E-payments	✓	✓	✗	✗
Regulatory fragmentation and regulatory arbitrage	Transparency[a]	✓ −	✓ +	✓ +	✓ −
	Express shipments[a]	✓	✓	✓	✓
	Fintech and regulatory tech cooperation	✓ +	✓ −	✗	✗
Crosscutting Issues					
Inclusivity and digital divide	Access to and use of internet[a]	✓ −	✓ −	✓ +	✓ +
	Digital inclusion	✗	✓	✗	✗
	Interconnection charges[a]	✓ −	✗	✓ +	✓ +
	Stakeholder engagement	✓ +	✗	✗	✓ −
Digital development	Data innovation	✓	✓	✗	✗
	Submarine cable[a]	✓ +	✗	✓ −	✓ −
Digitalization of big and small enterprises	SMEs[a]	✓ +	✓ +	✓ −	✓ −
Green digitalization	Paperless trading	✓ +	✓ +	✓ −	✓ −

✗ No provision   ✓ Identical or nearly identical provisions   ✓ − Less comprehensive provision   ✓ + More comprehensive provision

AI = artificial intelligence, ASDEA = Australia–Singapore Digital Economy Agreement, DEPA = Digital Economy Partnership Agreement, CPTPP = Comprehensive and Progressive Agreement for Trans-Pacific Partnership, RCEP = Regional Comprehensive Economic Partnership, SMEs = small and medium-sized enterprises.

[a] The CPTPP and the RCEP cover these topics in separate chapters other than the chapter on e-commerce.

Source: Study team analysis of agreement texts.

Tourism Sector as the Focal Point of Digital Regional Cooperation

In many instances, digitalization requires collective action to ensure successful outcomes. For example, in mobile payment innovations, decisions and resources are required from banks, payment service providers, telecom operators, and the public at large. Collective action exists nationally and regionally. Stakeholders have to be incentivized to take the appropriate action. In digitalization, they should perceive and understand the benefits of adopting the new technology.

One issue to consider is whether the tourism sector can be a laboratory to demonstrate the need for collective action in digitalization. This is related to its possible role as a focal point of regional cooperation in digitalization. Policymakers can design projects and programs that will facilitate requirements such as connectivity, skills development, cybersecurity, and data sharing. To make the policies and benefits more concrete, they can be applied to a specific sector, and tourism is a prime candidate.

A distinct advantage of using the tourism sector as a laboratory for regional cooperation is the main areas of digital transformation—process transformation, business model transformation, domain transformation, cultural or organizational digital transformation—which all figure prominently in the tourism value chain. In addition, as shown in Chapter 2, the entire tourism value chain is disposed to being digitized. Since the tourism sector has strong forward and backward linkages with the rest of the economy, its digitalization can readily create spillover effects and pull lagging sectors into the smart tourism ecosystem. For example, food suppliers will discover that it would be more efficient to deal with a digitalized tourism industry if they themselves adopt the same level of technology (Box 3).

Box 3: Strengthening Agriculture Value Chains in the Lao People's Democratic Republic through Tourism

After an extended period of subsistence farming, reforms have made agricultural production in the Lao People's Democratic Republic (Lao PDR) more market-oriented and diversified in the last few decades. As a result, the dominance of rice has been reduced and it now covers only half of the cropland, and its contribution to the value of total agricultural production has gone down to 20%. Meanwhile, the shares of vegetable and livestock production values are both at 20%. These shares are expected to grow but the challenge is to identify and establish value chains for vegetables and livestock. Tourism enterprises could be part of these value chains as they provide high-quality and high-value products to domestic and international tourists.

Meanwhile, the lack of reliable and affordable Internet service providers has inhibited the progress of e-commerce in the Lao PDR. More specific e-commerce laws are still largely under consideration, leaving the sector at a virtual standstill. An important initiative was making the agriculture sector part of the "e-strategy" developed to help boost demand for the country's products and services through domestic value chains. The platform links together food value-chain players alongside local government units and entrepreneurs through the use of mobile e-market services. For example, fintech solutions have enabled local government units to monitor prices of food items and basic household commodities during the pandemic.

Digitalization has enabled tourism enterprises to expand their market and improve their competitiveness and productivity. Based on an Asian Development Bank survey, it was determined that enterprises with web presence are associated with higher levels of occupancy. However, many micro, small, and medium-sized tourism enterprises have limited access to knowledge and skills, finance, and infrastructure. Traditional business owners may have an aversion to new technology or may perceive it as risky and not beneficial. This can be managed by doing demonstration projects that provide hands-on experience to raise awareness on the benefits of digital technology. By promoting digitalization in the tourism sector, firms can participate more effectively in the agriculture value chain. The likely sequence of events would be more digitalized tourism enterprises (e.g., hotels and restaurants), followed by more regular interaction with the agriculture value chain, and then greater incentive to accelerate e-strategy in the agriculture sector.

Source: Asian Development Bank. 2021. *Developing Agriculture and Tourism for Inclusive Growth in the Lao People's Democratic Republic*. Manila.

Conclusion

Regional cooperation has been an important tool in economic development. It is now extending from traditional areas of cooperation over trade and investment to the digital economy. For an emerging issue such as the digital economy, regional cooperation is of value to countries as they learn from each other's best practices. Moreover, regional commitments by countries enable them to push for domestic reforms and benefit from opportunities offered by digitalization of services.

Meanwhile, cross-border movement, such as in the tourism sector, highlights the issue of data flows and with it the debate about the need for a global or regional regulation to address related issues of data sharing, cybersecurity, and data sovereignty. Comparing some of the new agreements, it is found that a digital-only agreement is more comprehensive in nature to promote cross-border cooperation in digital economy. These include ASDEA and DEPA. This implies that the tourism sector of these economies has greater chances of benefiting from the emerging opportunities of digitalization. Given that the tourism sector has a spillover effect, it also implies that the participating countries in the digital agreements have greater potential for economy-wide benefit. The next chapter presents recommendations on how appropriate policies can be crafted, with the tourism sector as the main driver of regional cooperation in digitalization.

5 Policy Recommendations for Strengthening Regional Cooperation to Enable Smart Tourism

This chapter consolidates three major threads of analysis: (i) the stages of digital development, (ii) the degree of digitalization of the tourism sector, and (iii) the various issues that have to be addressed in the process of digitalization at a regional level. The frameworks presented in Chapter 1 (Figure 5) and Chapter 2 can be combined as the interface of the stage of digital transformation and the degree of digitalization of the tourism industry. Such interaction will largely determine the required policies, both at the national and regional levels, to deal with the issues enumerated in the PECC primer (PECC 2021). This chapter focuses on the regional measures. A list of policy recommendations relevant at the regional level are presented and discussed in this chapter.

Context of Framing the Policy Recommendations

The COVID-19 pandemic hit tourism harder than many other sectors, impacting incomes, livelihoods, public services, and economic opportunities in all continents. Tourist arrivals worldwide fell by 72% in 2020, with Asia and the Pacific recording the largest regional decline. Digitalization has emerged as an important tool to strengthen both the tourism sector's recovery and the long-term agenda of making it more resilient, inclusive, and sustainable.

Regional organizations, such as ASEAN, and their member countries have agreed that the pandemic should serve as an impetus and opportunity for the sector to build back better by designing and building a more sustainable tourism sector that would underpin its resilience (ERIA 2022). Use of digital technology and supportive government policies encouraging public and private sectors to adopt digitally driven tourism practices have therefore been gaining importance.

The tourism sector can be a major beneficiary of the thrust of using digitalization to build back better. A key finding of Chapter 2 is that the entire tourism value chain is disposed to technology upgrading. This is consistent with the observation that the tourism sector can utilize big data and analytics to achieve more sustainable tourism management and recovery. Moreover, compared to other sectors, the amount of consumer personal data involved in business operations is significantly larger in tourism, a highly information-intensive industry. Meanwhile, Chapter 3 showed the large disparity among ASEAN member countries on their stage of digitalization and readiness for smart tourism. National policies and programs to narrow the digital divide are important. Many of the regional groupings have formulated aspirations for smart tourism practices among their member countries. Hence, uneven development across and within countries should be seen as opportunities for regional cooperation in digital regulations and issues. Countries can adopt coherent digital rules, thus increasing competitiveness for greater integration in goods, services, and factors markets.

The previous chapter aimed to answer the most critical research question of this study: "What are the gaps and challenges in regional cooperation in digital economy agreements for these to facilitate a regional (smart tourism ecosystem)?" As explained in Chapter 3 and Chapter 4, data governance and regulatory fragmentation at the regional level are particularly important for the tourism sector. This chapter presents policy recommendations that can deal with gaps and challenges.

The majority of the policy recommendations are initiatives and focus areas outlined by different regional groupings related to the digital economy and trade. It is evident that DEPA, ASDEA, RCEP, and CPTPP are harbingers of change in the landscape of regional collaboration in digital economy. Some issues have not been adequately addressed by these digital agreements and require concerted action in the future. The following subchapter recommends policies for these issues that can be considered by future bilateral and multilateral agreements. By leveraging the collective infrastructure, tools, and capabilities of the digital economy, tourism stakeholders can improve efficiency, enhance customer experiences, personalize offerings, and adapt to the evolving needs and expectations of modern travelers.

Policy Recommendations to Strengthen Pillars of Smart Tourism

1. Data Protection and Privacy

The tourism industry deals with large amounts of data, with businesses, such as travel agencies and hotels, and governments collecting information at each step of the tourists' journey. These include personal and confidential data, which makes them a potential target for cybercriminals. According to a study, only 24% of consumers in the travel industry spend time in implementing additional security measures.[26] This makes it imperative that the data are well protected and provided to authorized parties only on user's consent.

Cryptography. As the science of encoding and decoding information, cryptography plays a vital role in promoting digitalization by ensuring secure and confidential communication, safeguarding critical infrastructure, and maintaining trust in digital transactions. Few of the policy recommendations in this regard are

(i) **Strengthening encryption standards through multistakeholder collaboration and legislative protection.** To foster digitalization and protect confidential information, it is crucial to support the development and use of robust encryption algorithms and standards. Governments should encourage collaboration with technology experts, researchers, and cryptographic communities to ensure encryption algorithms remain secure against emerging threats. Additionally, policymakers should refrain from introducing legislation that mandates weakened encryption, as it would undermine data security and trust in digital systems.

(ii) **Promoting encryption education and awareness.** Governments should invest in educational programs and awareness campaigns to promote understanding and responsible use of encryption. By empowering individuals, businesses, and organizations with knowledge about

---

[26] *Thales Group.* 2022. Lack of Consumer Trust Across Industries to Protect Their Personal Data, New Research from Thales Has Revealed. 3 October. https://www.thalesgroup.com/en/countries-europe/romania/press_release/lack-consumer-trust-across-industries-protect-their-personal.

encryption technologies, they can make informed decisions on protecting their digital assets and data. This can include initiatives such as workshops, training programs, and awareness campaigns to emphasize the importance of encryption in maintaining privacy and security. For instance, the European Union Agency for Cybersecurity runs awareness campaigns to disseminate and promote its work in the cybersecurity field, including cryptography, and to educate stakeholders and the public on the regulatory developments and latest technologies.[27]

(iii) **Harmonizing relevant policies and standards that impact encryption.** Regional cooperation can help harmonize encryption policies, facilitate cross-border data transfers, and promote trust in digital transactions across nations. Governments should actively engage in international forums, such as standardization bodies and intergovernmental organizations, to establish global guidelines and standards for cryptographic practices. For example, governments can adhere to "ISO/IEC 18033 series" jointly developed by the International Organization for Standardization (ISO) and the International Electrotechnical Commission, which specifies encryption systems for the purpose of data confidentiality.[28]

(iv) **Balancing security and privacy.** Regional cooperation should facilitate a balance between security and privacy concerns. While strong encryption is crucial for safeguarding digital assets, it is important to address legitimate law enforcement and national security needs. Governments should collaborate with technology companies to explore solutions that enable lawful access to encrypted data while preserving the overall security and privacy of individuals and organizations.

(v) **Protecting freedom of choice of ICT products in using cryptography.** Governments should recognize that individual entities have freedom to choose the cryptography algorithm and trade independently without partnering with a local entity. To ensure this, governments should not require manufacturer or supplier of ICT goods using cryptography to disclose any proprietary information relating to cryptography, nor require manufacturer or supplier to partner with a local person in its territory, nor use a particular cryptographic algorithm as a necessary condition for trade. DEPA, for example, has a clause on cryptography, which requires governments to adhere to the above conditions.

2. Intellectual Property

Intellectual property (IP) systems provide a regulatory framework aiming to foster innovation and creativity and enabling people and companies to earn recognition or benefit financially. Because of these reasons, IP systems have emerged as one of the key drivers of growth in tourism. IP rights in tourism have various benefits, such as enhancing management of companies and tourism destinations, differentiating tourism destinations and products from competitors, and attracting investment and financing especially for SMEs (WIPO and UNWTO 2021).

Source Code. Protecting source code is crucial as it safeguards IP rights, encourages innovation, and ensures the security and integrity of digital systems. Few of the policy recommendations in this regard are listed below:

---

[27]   European Union Agency for Cybersecurity. Awareness Raising. https://www.enisa.europa.eu/topics/cybersecurity-education.

[28]   International Organization for Standardization (ISO). ISO/IEC 18033-1:2021: Information Security – Encryption Algorithms – Part 1: General. https://www.iso.org/standard/76156.html.

(i)   **Strengthening intellectual property protection through legislative actions.** Regional cooperation should facilitate governments in enacting laws and regulations explicitly recognizing source code as IP and provide legal protection against unauthorized copying, distribution, and modification. This includes enforcing copyright laws and considering additional measures, like trade secret protection for proprietary source code. For instance, the European Union law - Directive 2009/24 EC on the legal protection of computer programs protects the source code as literary works.[29]

(ii)   **Creating mechanisms to ensure strict enforcement of Nondisclosure Agreements.** Nondisclosure agreements help protect source code as confidential information and provide legal remedies in case of unauthorized disclosure or misuse. Regional groupings should enable member nations to create necessary regulatory frameworks to enforce and uphold non-disclosure agreements between parties involved in the development, distribution, or licensing of source code. In addition, governments should not require transfer of or access to the source code of a software owned by parties of another country as a necessary condition for trade.

(iii) **Encouraging secure code collaboration platforms.** Regional groupings can also support the development and adoption of secure code collaboration platforms enabling developers to work together while protecting the confidentiality of source code. These platforms should incorporate encryption, access controls, and secure communication channels to ensure that source code remains protected during collaboration.

3. Consumer Protection

In a digital economy, most of the interactions between consumers and businesses are conducted online. As a result, digital consumers face challenges such as misleading ratings or reviews, scams, and fraud (OECD 2021). These issues can make consumers lose trust in online marketplaces and e-commerce. The tourism industry is most vulnerable to fraud, with digital scams in travel and leisure industry rising by approximately 111% during 2019–2021 (TransUnion 2022).

Safe Online Environment. Maintaining a safe online environment in the digital economy is essential for building trust, protecting user data, and fostering secure transactions, enabling businesses and individuals to thrive in the digital ecosystem:

(i)   **Creation of incident response and reporting mechanisms.** Regional groupings should assist governments in creating incident response frameworks that enable timely reporting and mitigation of online threats faced by users. This includes establishing reporting channels for individuals and organizations to report cyber incidents, as well as providing support and guidance on incident response and recovery. For instance, ASEAN countries have their own Computer Emergency Response Teams (CERTs) handling computer security incidents. For example, SingCERT in Singapore, VNCERT in Viet Nam, etc.

(ii)   **Encouraging multistakeholder collaboration.** Regional cooperation mechanisms should adopt a multistakeholder approach and collaborate with industrial, government, and global stakeholders to address issues affecting online safety and security. As an illustration, governments should adhere to guidelines released by international agencies like "Consumer Protection in E-Commerce" by OECD and "Consumers International Guidelines for Online Product Safety" by Consumers International.

---

[29]   P. Szwed. 2022. How Are Computer Programs Protected in Europe: Copyright or Patent Protection? *Discover Digital Law*. 23 January. https://discoverdigitallaw.com/how-are-computer-programs-protected-in-europe-copyright-or-patent-protection/.

4. Digital Identity

Digital identities have a tremendous potential in the tourism sector. From a tourist's point of view, it makes travel seamless, secure, and safe. Governments and businesses can also benefit from secure screening and identification of travelers. Many countries have already implemented one form of digital ID or ePassport. However, there is still scope for collaboration between countries to benefit from making interoperable systems across multiple sectors.

Digital Identity. Digital identity systems have the potential to enable economic value creation by increasing inclusivity, providing greater access to goods and services, increasing formalization, reducing frauds, protecting rights, and increasing transparency.[30] Some of the policy recommendation in this regard are the following:

(i)   **Promoting interoperability and compatibility of digital ID systems.** Regional groupings should enable member nations to collaborate and promote interoperability and compatibility of their respective digital ID systems. The most critical element is harmonization of digital ID standards. For example, the "Catalogue of Technical Standards for Digital Identification Systems" developed by World Bank provides standards for different types of digital identities. Another important aspect is to establish legal frameworks and standards for governing the use of digital identities, including identity verification, authentication, and data protection. The laws and regulations should also provide legal protection to identity systems of other countries.

(ii)   **Promoting inclusion and accessibility.** Governments should ensure that digital identity solutions are inclusive and accessible to all members of society. Policies should be in place to address issues such as digital divide, affordability, literacy, and language barriers. Governments should also consider alternative authentication methods for individuals who may not have traditional identity documents.

5. Data Sharing

Data is an important resource for economic growth, competitiveness, job creation, and societal progress.[31] Maintaining open datasets can benefit multiple stakeholders, from small to big businesses or organizations, by opening new and equal opportunities. Various regions like Europe have already implemented open data portals, which provide datasets on various sectors including tourism.[32]

Open Government Data. Open government data referring to the public data freely available and accessible to the public is vital in terms of promoting transparency, encouraging innovation, and enabling data-driven solutions to promote economic growth and improve public services. Some of the policy recommendations in this regard are as follows:

(i)   **Developing open-data policies.** Regional groupings should encourage member countries to establish clear policies and guidelines that promote the release of government data in open and machine-readable formats. While making the data available, regional groupings should

---

[30]   McKinsey Global Institute. 2019. *Digital Identification: A Key to Inclusive Growth*. https://www.mckinsey.com/capabilities/mckinsey-digital/our-insights/digital-identification-a-key-to-inclusive-growth.

[31]   European Commission. A European Strategy for Data. https://digital-strategy.ec.europa.eu/en/policies/strategy-data.

[32]   European Commission. Eurostat. EU Tourism Database. https://ec.europa.eu/eurostat/web/tourism/data/database (accessed July 2023).

encourage governments to maintain privacy, anonymize the data, provide a descriptive metadata, and make it available in a machine-readable format that could be searched, retrieved, used, reused, and distributed. For instance, the European Open Data Directive, which entered into force in 2019, mandates the release of public sector data in free and open formats.[33]

(ii)   **Maintaining accessible data portals.** Regional cooperation mechanisms should facilitate member countries to ensure that open government data are easily discoverable and accessible to the public. This includes providing user-friendly data portals, Application Programme Interfaces, and search tools that enable efficient access and retrieval of data. Regional groupings should also encourage the use of open standards and data formats to facilitate interoperability and integration with other datasets and should regularly update the datasets. For example, Asia Open Data Partnership, which includes 19 partners from 11 economies, has established Dataportal.asia, which harvests metadata from different open datasets in different regions across Asia. As of October 2023, it provides over 185,000 datasets.[34]

6. Quality of Service

Ensuring delivery of quality service is important for maintaining higher levels of customer satisfaction. Even in the digital economy, this matters as tourists will prefer products or services with better quality. For example, tourists will prefer travel agents who offer smooth booking experience over one providing poor service.

Standards and Conformity Assessment. This assessment is crucial in the digital economy as they ensure interoperability, compatibility, and trust among digital products and services, facilitating seamless integration, innovation, and market growth. Few of the policy recommendations in this regard are as follows:

(i)   **Promoting adoption of international standards.** Regional groupings should encourage governments to adopt internationally recognized standards in the digital economy, like the "UNCITRAL Model Law on Electronic Commerce" by the United Nations and the World Trade Organization's rules and principles on digital trade. PPPs will be key to bringing diverse expertise, fostering innovation, and ensuring that standards meet the needs of both industry and society.

(ii)   **Harmonizing regulatory requirements.** Harmonization of regulatory requirements helps to reduce barriers to trade, minimize duplication of testing, and streamline market access for digital products and services. Regional groups should strive for harmonization of regulatory requirements across member countries. For example, the ASEAN Digital Trade Standards and Conformance Working Group works toward promoting harmonization, standardization, and conformity assessment of digital trade in ASEAN. One of its objectives includes identifying areas for harmonizing standards, regulations, technical requirements, and procedures.[35]

---

[33]   Government of Ireland, Department of Public Expenditure and Reform. Open Data Directive. https://data.gov.ie/pages/open-data-directive.

[34]   Dataportal.asia. https://dataportal.asia/about/dpa.

[35]   ASEAN Digital Trade Standards and Conformance Working Group. 2019. Terms of Reference. https://www.tisi.go.th/data/interstandard/pdf/asean/asean_dtscwg_tor_2_10.pdf.

7. Artificial Intelligence

Artificial intelligence (AI) presents huge opportunities for tourists, businesses, and governments, with applications like chatbots, predictive analysis, personalized experience, and automation. Despite these benefits, AI still faces regulatory challenges because of the unpredictable nature of business models relying on these technologies, data privacy, security, ownership, and control issues, and AI's complex nature as opposed to traditional software.[36]

Artificial Intelligence and Emerging Technologies. AI and emerging technologies drive automation, improve efficiency, and encourage innovation, leading to new business opportunities, improved user experience, and transformed industries across various sectors. A policy recommendation in this regard is

- **Developing ethical and responsible regulatory frameworks for artificial intelligence governance.** Regional groupings should encourage member countries to establish regulatory frameworks that address the unique challenges posed by AI and emerging technologies. These frameworks should guide the development, deployment, and use of artificial intelligence systems. Regional groups should ensure that the regulations of these technologies should be risk-based while focusing on the probability and severity of the potential harm. These frameworks should also address issues such as transparency, fairness, accountability, and the prevention of discriminatory outcomes. Regional groups should actively promote international collaboration on global and regional forums, sharing best practices, and contributing to the development of international standards and guidelines.

8. Cross-Border Data Flows

Cross-border data flows are essential to economic growth in the digital economy, including for tourism. Restrictions on cross-border data flows including data localization measures could be based on legitimate concerns on privacy and data protection, yet can still pose risks of hindering cross-border data flows, increasing cost for companies, and limiting innovation. Some of the policy recommendations to address this challenge are given below:

- (i) **Following risk-based approaches to data localization requirement.** Rather than imposing restrictions on all kinds of financial data, regional groupings should urge governments to adopt risk-based approaches to data localization, considering the sensitivity and criticality of financial data. This includes identifying specific types of data or functions that require localization and allowing flexibility for nonsensitive data or low-risk operations.
- (ii) **Providing regulatory clarity and certainty.** Financial institutions can make informed decisions and implement necessary measures to comply with the regulations, if the regulations and standards are clear. Thus, regional groupings should encourage governments to establish clear guidelines, regulations, and standards to specify the conditions, scope, and processes related to data localization requirements.

---

[36] *Digital Regulation Platform.* 2020. Elements of Spectrum Management for Upcoming Technologies. 2 September. https://digitalregulation.org/3004297–2/e.

9. Digital Trade Standards

Digital trade standards ensure interoperability among different digital platforms and enable smooth integration of diverse services for an enhanced tourist experience. The standardization also secures data transmission, thereby building trust in digital transactions and encouraging more tourists to adopt the smart tourism services.

E-invoicing. Defined as the electronic exchange of invoice data between buyers and suppliers, e-invoicing enables businesses to streamline their invoicing processes, reduce costs, and contribute to the overall digital transformation of the economy. Some of the policy recommendations in this regard are listed below:

(i)   **Strengthening standardization and interoperability.** For fast paced digitalization, regional groupings must strengthen collaboration of national governments to establish clear standards and formats for e-invoicing that are compatible across different systems and industries. This will ensure seamless communication between buyers and suppliers and avoids the need for multiple invoicing platforms. Moreover, regional groupings must encourage use of open standards to facilitate widespread adoption.

(ii)   **Promoting integration with business systems.** Regional groupings should concur on integration of e-invoicing systems with other business processes and systems, such as accounting software and enterprise resource planning systems. Governments should consider uniform business interoperability specifications across a defined list of preferred accounting and enterprise resource planning platforms in predecided formats. This integration streamlines invoicing procedures, reduces errors, and enhances overall efficiency.

(iii) **Mandating or incentivizing adoption.** Regional groupings should collaborate to implement a mandatory e-invoicing requirement for businesses above a certain turnover threshold to accelerate the adoption of e-invoicing and drive standardization. They can launch e-invoicing networks, like InvoiceNow in Singapore and E-Faktur in Indonesia, backed by a clearance model. Alternatively, national governments can be supported to roll out financial incentives, such as tax benefits or grants, that can be provided to encourage businesses to adopt e-invoicing voluntarily.

E-payments. E-payments, electronic transactions conducted through digital platforms that enable the transfer of funds between parties, can eliminate the need for traditional paper-based payment methods, thereby ensuring transparency and accountability. Some of the policy recommendations in this regard are listed below:

(i)   **Investing in digital payment infrastructure.** Regional groupings must work toward secure payment gateways, interoperable systems, and real-time payment settlement mechanisms. Governments should actively collaborate with payment service providers, banks, and technology companies to enhance the reliability, speed, and accessibility of digital payment systems.

(ii)   **Strengthening interoperability and standardization.** Regional groupings should concur on rationalization of standards of e-payment systems to ensure seamless integration between different payment platforms and service providers. Regional groupings can engage in multilateral agreements, which enable information sharing between regulatory authorities, referral of qualified firms to other jurisdictions, and commitments to explore joint projects related to fintech innovation based on common standards. For instance, Bank Negara Malaysia and the Monetary Authority of Singapore have launched a cross-border QR code payment linkage between their individual payment systems, which allow customers to make retail payments by scanning QR codes.[37]

(iii) **Harmonizing regulatory framework for payments.** Regional groupings must work toward a comprehensive regulatory framework, which is flexible, technology-neutral, and adaptive to evolving payment technologies. Governments should be encouraged to align their (anti-money laundering and/or combating the financing of Terrorism) legal framework with the Financial Action Task Force standards and focus on basing their payment system principles to facilitate financial inclusion without undermining financial integrity, customer identification, and verification regulations.

10. Regulatory Fragmentation

The lack of harmonization between regulations and laws leads to slower adoption of smart tourism practices and technologies, as businesses will hesitate to invest in sectors and regions having complex and conflicting regulations. The inconsistency in legal frameworks results in higher compliance costs and administrative burdens, thereby impeding innovation and hindering collaboration between regions.

Fintech and Regulatory Tech Cooperation. Fintech (the use of technology to provide innovative financial products, services, and solutions), and Regulatory tech (application of technology to facilitate regulatory compliance and improve regulatory processes)enhance efficiency, accessibility, and convenience in financial services, while introducing new business models and disrupting traditional financial systems. Some of the policy recommendations in this regard are listed below:

(i) **Establishing regulatory sandboxes for cross-border testing.** Regional groupings should facilitate cross-border testing of fintech and regulatory tech solutions by establishing international regulatory sandboxes or mutual recognition frameworks. This will allow companies to test their products in multiple jurisdictions, promoting global interoperability and reducing regulatory barriers. For instance, ASEAN has introduced the Regulatory Pilot Space initiative to give businesses the certainty that the data handlingcross the border complies with ASEAN Framework on Personal Data protection.[38]

(ii) **Promoting regulatory agility.** Regional groupings should prompt national governments to regularly review and update existing regulations to keep pace with technological advancements. The emphasis should be on implementing flexible and principles-based regulations that accommodate innovation and promote competition while safeguarding consumer interests. For instance, OECD has developed the Services Trade Restrictiveness Index to track the agility of the regulatory environment in the APEC region and find areas, which can be discussed by regional groupings, to identify best practices in priority sectors.

(iii) **Supporting proportional regulation.** Regional groupings should advocate proportional and risk-based regulations that consider the size and complexity of fintech and regulatory tech firms. Cumbersome regulations that may stifle innovation, particularly for start-ups and smaller players should be avoided. For example, governments must try to ensure that businesses are not subject to local presence requirements, whether it be establishing or

---

37 *Bank Negara Malaysia.* 2023. Launch of Cross-border QR Code Payments Connectivity between Malaysia and Singapore. 31 March. https://www.bnm.gov.my/-/qrcode-connectivity-my-sg.

38 GSMA. 2019. *ASEAN Regulatory Pilot Space for Cross-Border Data Flows.* Summary presentation of the White Paper of the same title. 7 November. https://www.gsma.com/asia-pacific/wp-content/uploads/2019/11/ASEAN-RPS-November-2019-v2.pdf.

maintaining a representative office, being a resident in a country, or meeting onerous local shareholding requirements, as a prerequisite for the cross-border supply of goods and services to that country.

11. Inclusivity and Digital Divide

Focus on inclusivity and bridging the digital divide improves accessibility to information, encourages community participation, and establishes a sustainable tourism environment. Strategies like expanding connectivity infrastructure, providing digital skills training, fostering digital innovation, and designing user-friendly interfaces can address the digital divide among citizens and tourists.

Digital Inclusion. This ensures that all individuals have access to and can fully participate in the digital world. Some of the policy recommendations in this regard are listed below:

(i)   **Developing the digital infrastructure.** Regional groupings must collaborate on establishing robust digital infrastructure, including high-speed Internet connectivity, particularly in underserved areas. They can cooperate to accelerate network infrastructure construction and facilitate interconnection. They should promote the installation of Internet Exchange Points, which can make Internet access central to development and growth initiatives.

(ii)   **Providing local content and multilingual support.** Regional groupings should facilitate creation and dissemination of local content in diverse languages to cater to the needs of different communities. They should ensure that digital platforms and services support multiple languages, making them more inclusive and accessible to individuals with limited proficiency in the dominant language.

(iii)   **Establishing digital inclusion metrics and monitoring.** Regional groupings must concur on metrics and indicators to track progress in digital inclusion initiatives. Data on digital access, usage, and skills should be observed for evidence-based decision-making. Regional groupings can encourage governments to carry out evaluation of the effectiveness of policies and programs for identification of gaps and adjustment of strategies as needed. For instance, EDISON Alliance under the World Economic Forum has launched a new tool to share best practices in expanding digital inclusion, the Digital Inclusion Navigator.[39]

Stakeholder Engagement. Stakeholder engagement for digital inclusion includes active involvement and collaboration of government agencies, private sector organizations, civil society groups, community-based organizations, academic institutions, and individuals themselves to promote and advance digital inclusion initiatives. Some of the policy recommendations in this regard are listed below:

(i)   **Supporting multistakeholder platforms.** Regional groupings should facilitate dedicated platforms or working groups, including multiple stakeholders focused on digital inclusion. These platforms can bring together representatives from government, private sector organizations, civil society groups, academia, and individuals to collaborate, exchange knowledge, and coordinate efforts.

---

[39]   United Nations Development Programme. 2022. Digital Inclusion Navigator: A Platform to Help Bridge Digital Divide for Billions. Blog. 24 May. https://www.undp.org/blog/digital-inclusion-navigator-platform-help-bridge-digital-divide-billions.

(ii)   **Encouraging participation of grassroots organizations and communities.** Regional groupings must motivate grassroots organizations, community-based groups, and local representatives to be involved in digital inclusion initiatives. These organizations have close connections with the communities they serve and can provide valuable insights into the specific needs and challenges faced by marginalized populations.

(iii)   **Strengthening early capacity building.** Regional groupings should facilitate workshops, seminars, and training sessions to enhance stakeholders' knowledge and skills in utilizing digital technologies for inclusive development. Regional groupings should strengthen the readiness of public servants, citizens, and businesses for Digital Government through use of digital tools. These groupings must facilitate governments to invest in the use of technology in primary and secondary education as well as in nonformal education, including in libraries, museums, and other community-based organizations to reduce disparities between income levels and promote development of a workforce for the digital economy.

12. Digital Development

Digital development has transformed smart tourism by empowering travelers with information, convenience, personalization, and immersive experiences, thereby enabling smart destinations and smart travel. It provides tourists end-to-end assistance from trip planning, booking, and reservations using personalized recommendations. On the supply side, businesses can adapt and offer innovative services with the help of big data analytics to make data-driven decisions for higher personalization. This segment covers issues like data governance framework, open data initiatives, ethical and responsible data use, and data impact assessment. Policy recommendations related to these issues have been discussed under various headings above.

APPENDIXES

Table A1: Data Matrix for All Indicators for Countries' Level of Readiness for Smart Tourism

Principle	Subprinciple	Parameters	Subparameter	Final Score									Source	Link	Year	Access date
				INO	THA	SIN	VIE	MAL	PHI	CAM	BRU	LAO				
Attractiveness	Smart Attraction	Digital visiting	Official Tourist app	0	100	100	0	100	100	100	100	0	Individual websites	1. Thailand: https://www.tourismthailand.org/Plan-Your-Trip/Essential-Application 2. https://www.visitsingapore.com/travel-guide-tips/visit-singapore-travel-guide-app/ 3. Malaysia: https://app.philippines.travel/ 4. Philippines: https://app.philippines.travel/ 5. Cambodia: https://www.phnompenhpost.com/national/ministry-launches-visit-cambodia-website-app 6. Brunei Darussalam: https://www.bruneitourism.com/	2023	30 Mar 2023
		City Attractiveness	Smart City Projects	0	1	4	0	4	0	3	100	7	ASEAN	https://asean.org/wp-content/uploads/2022/10/2022-ASCN-ME-Report-Final_21Sep2022-for-public.pdf	2022	NA
		Cost of staying in a country	Hotel price index	100	10	9	0	56	40	14	...	35	WEF TTDI	https://www.weforum.org/reports/travel-and-tourism-development-index-2021/explore-the-data/	2021	30 Mar 2023
			Purchasing power parity	68	51	0	73	49	47	65	24	87	World Bank	https://databank.worldbank.org/source/world-development-indicators#	2021	2 Apr 2023
		Destination attractiveness	Number of world heritage sites	100	67	11	89	44	67	33	0	33	UNESCO	https://whc.unesco.org/en/list/stat/	2023	2 Apr 2023
			International inbound tourists	0	5	33	1	10	0	3	100	6	UNWTO dashboard	https://www.unwto.org/tourism-data/global-and-regional-tourism-performance	2019	29 Mar 2023
			International tourism expenditure	70	100	65	39	37	86	48	0	10	UNWTO dashboard	https://www.unwto.org/tourism-data/global-and-regional-tourism-performance	2019	29 Mar 2023
	Smart Amenities	Availability of hotels	Hotel infrastructure (Number of hotels and rooms)	100	26	0	87	7	30	29	0	35	UNWTO dashboard	https://www.unwto.org/tourism-data/global-and-regional-tourism-performance	2020	29 Mar 2023
				100	36	5	66	16	37	21	0	20	UNWTO dashboard	https://www.unwto.org/tourism-data/global-and-regional-tourism-performance	2020	29 Mar 2023
		Efficient use of resources for a tech-enabled and customized experience	Free public Wi-Fi	100	9	1	33	3	24	10	0	2	Wi-Fi Map	https://www.wifimap.io/countries	2023	2 Apr 2023
			Free hotel Wi-Fi	29	66	87	58	0	27	65	100	59	Booking.com	https://www.booking.com/	2023	15 Mar 2023

continued on next page

Table A1 *continued*

Principle	Subprinciple	Parameters	Subparameter	Final Score									Source	Link	Year	Access date
				INO	THA	SIN	VIE	MAL	PHI	CAM	BRU	LAO				
		E-commerce and ticketing	Online Merchant Payment	0	65	100	20	74	5	…	…	…	World Bank	https://www.worldbank.org/en/publication/globalfindex	2021	3 Apr 2023
			UNCTAD B2C E-commerce index	37	74	100	53	81	29	10	…	24	UNCTAD B2C E-Commerce Index 202	https://unctad.org/system/files/official-document/tn_unctad_ict4d17_en.pdf	2020	NA
		Other	Car rental facilities	0	100	80	20	60	100	60	…	40	WEF TTDI	https://www.weforum.org/reports/travel-and-tourism-development-index-2021/explore-the-data	2021	30 Mar 2023
			Number of ATMs	41	100	47	20	47	22	24	65	21	World Bank	https://data.worldbank.org/indicator/FB.ATM.TOTL.P5	2021	29 Apr 2023
	Smart Content	Visibility of country's tourism board online	Country branding strategy rating	100	13	33	33	80	40	0	…	7	WEF TTDI	https://www.weforum.org/reports/travel-and-tourism-development-index-2021/explore-the-data/	2021	30 Mar 2023
			Interactivity on the Tourism website	100	100	100	100	0	100	100	100	0	Tourism board directory	https://www.brinzan.com/promoting-tourism-all-country-tourism-board-websites-in-the-world/	2023	30 Mar 2023
	Online Popularity	Digital demand	Natural tourism	22	100	25	37	18	28	11	…	0	WEF TTDI	https://www.weforum.org/reports/travel-and-tourism-development-index-2021/explore-the-data/	2021	30 Mar 2023
			Cultural and Entertainment Tourism	19	89	100	61	29	27	24	…	0	WEF TTDI	https://www.weforum.org/reports/travel-and-tourism-development-index-2021/explore-the-data/	2021	30 Mar 2023
		Social media presence	Presence on Instagram (Followers and posts)	100	8	53	19	10	4	0	7	14	Follow-up on links provided in Directory	https://www.brinzan.com/promoting-tourism-all-country-tourism-board-websites-in-the-world/	2023	4 Apr 2023
				100	48	30	28	82	25	0	10	2				4 Apr 2023
			Presence on Twitter	80	2	3	0	12	100	0	…	3	Twitter	https://www.brinzan.com/promoting-tourism-all-country-tourism-board-websites-in-the-world/	2023	4 Apr 2023
Accessibility	Smart Mobility	Ease of travelling to country	Visa friendliness	42	39	81	42	98	79	100	29	85	Passport Index	https://www.passportindex.org/byWelcomingRank.php	2023	4 Apr 2023
		Availability and quality of modes of transport	Air transport infrastructure (efficiency and connectivity)	43	54	100	32	54	0	4	…	0	WEF TTDI	https://www.weforum.org/reports/travel-and-tourism-development-index-2021/explore-the-data/	2021	30 Mar 2023
				100	83	54	80	63	61	22	…	0				
			Ground transport infrastructure (Quality of roads, efficiency of trail services, efficiency of public transport, adequate access to public transport)	59	31	100	22	56	0	6	…	13				
				77	42	100	63	73	27	0	…	0				
				64	21	100	30	39	0	9	…	6				
				58	26	100	39	42	19	0	…	16				
		Smartness of mobility in smart cities	Car sharing apps	36	51	32	100	45	0	…	…	…	IMD Smart Cities Index	https://www.imd.org/wp-content/uploads/2023/04/smartcityindex-2023-v7.pdf	2023	NA
			Smart parking	28	54	26	100	9	0	…	…	…				
			Bicycle hiring	39	100	40	50	0	29	…	…	…				
			Online ticket sales	94	82	0	100	82	5	…	…	…				
			Information availability	12	69	100	48	52	0	…	…	…				

continued on next page

Table A1 *continued*

Principle	Subprinciple	Parameters	Subparameter	Final Score									Source	Link	Year	Access date
				INO	THA	SIN	VIE	MAL	PHI	CAM	BRU	LAO				
	Smart Convenience	Ease of payments	Electronic payments	18	85	100	35	66	30	4	…	0	World Bank	https://www.worldbank.org/en/publication/globalfindex	2021	4 Apr 2023
		Ease of availing services	3G mobile network coverage	60	93	100	100	67	73	73	73	0	ITU Digital Development Dashboard	https://www.itu.int/en/ITU-D/Statistics/Dashboards/Pages/Digital-Development.aspx	2021	29 Mar 2023
			4G mobile network coverage	92	96	100	100	90	58	92	90	0	ITU Digital Development Dashboard	https://www.itu.int/en/ITU-D/Statistics/Dashboards/Pages/Digital-Development.aspx	2021	29 Mar 2023
			Internet quality (Mobile and fixed broadband download speed)	0	34	97	39	46	8	2	100	15	Speedtest by Ookla	https://www.speedtest.net/global-index	2023	29 Mar 2023
				3	84	100	33	35	33	1	14	5	Speedtest by Ookla	https://www.speedtest.net/global-index		29 Mar 2023
			Digital identities	100	100	100	0	100	0	0	…	0	World Bank	World Development Report: Data Regulations Diagnostic Survey	2021	29 Mar 2023
			Security of digital identity	100	100	100	100	100	100	0	0	0	ICAO	https://www.icao.int/Security/FAL/PKD/Pages/ICAO-PKDParticipants.aspx	2023	29 Mar 2023
			Use of digital platform for providing financial services	48	67	100	43	71	43	0	…	5	WEF TTDI	https://www.weforum.org/reports/travel-and-tourism-development-index-2021/explore-the-data/	2021	30 Mar 2023
			Use of digital platforms for providing transportation and shipping	74	53	100	42	63	16	11	…	0				
			Use of digital platforms for providing hotels, restaurants, and leisure activities services	75	81	100	69	56	25	19	…	0				
	Barrier-Free Designs	Inclusivity in the country	Economic inequality	69	31	100	14	44	0	0	75	18	World Economics	https://www.worldeconomics.com/Indicator-Data/Inequality/Gini-Coefficient.aspx	Different years for different economies	3 Apr 2023
			Gender equality	11	31	47	23	0	100	7	2	69	WEF	https://www3.weforum.org/docs/WEF_GGGR_2022.pdf	2020	NA
			Disability friendly	0	14	100	12	14	12	29	62	6	Booking.com	https://www.booking.com/	2023	15 Mar 2023

continued on next page

Table A1 *continued*

Principle	Subprinciple	Parameters	Subparameter	Final Score									Source	Link	Year	Access date
				INO	THA	SIN	VIE	MAL	PHI	CAM	BRU	LAO				
Sustainability	Life and Tourism Environment	Environmental sustainability (based on Tourism Sustainability Development Index)	CO2 emissions	21	28	23	25	7	100	49	0	11	Our World in Data	https://ourworldindata.org/explorers/co2?facet=entity&Gas+or+Warming=CO%E2%82%82&Accounting=Production-based&Fuel+or+Land+Use+Change=All+fossil+emissions&Count=Per+capita	2021	4 Apr 2023
			Water stress	2	3	0	5	29	3	100	29	21	World Bank	https://databank.worldbank.org/source/world-development-indicators#	2020	4 Apr 2023
			Air quality	0	20	37	3	21	30	78	100	3	IQAir	https://www.iqair.com/in-en/world-most-polluted-countries	2022	4 Apr 2023
			Vegetal forest cover	54	34	0	50	72	5	48	100	100	World Bank Forest Area database	https://data.worldbank.org/indicator/AG.LND.FRST.ZS	2020	4 Apr 2023
			Protected areas	10	37	0	2	17	4	100	22	55	Protected planet database	https://www.protectedplanet.net/en/search-areas?geo_type=country	2021	4 Apr 2023
		Digital skills gap	Digital skills institution	37	29	100	24	75	55	10	73	…	Wiley Digital Skills Gap Index	https://dsgi.wiley.com/global-rankings/	2021	2 Apr 2023
			Digital responsiveness	38	32	100	32	68	43	0	70	…				
			Government support	36	19	100	45	87	38	21	88	…				
			Supply, demand, and competitiveness	77	41	95	59	100	57	0	66	…				
			Data ethics and integrity	72	69	94	57	100	57	0	42	…				
			Academia Research intensity	60	66	100	88	95	50	12	50	…				
	City Resilience	Business resilience	Economic factors	29	19	100	16	44	32	14	64	0	2022 FM Global Resilience Index	https://www.fmglobal.com/research-and-resources/tools-and-resources/resilienceindex/explore-the-data/?&vd=1	2022	29 Mar 2023
			Risk quality factor	43	69	100	27	94	12	6	54	0				
			Supply chain factors	39	49	100	34	54	16	3	39	0				
		Cybersecurity	Cybersecurity risk	95	85	100	95	99	78	0	47	2	ITU Global Cybersecurity Index 2020	https://www.itu.int/epublications/publication/D-STR-GCI.01-2021-HTM-E#:~:text=The%20Global%20Cybersecurity%20Index%20(GCI,countries%20and%20other%20international%20organizations.	2020	4 Apr 2023
		Population Density	Population density	22	23	0	10	31	8	34	38	100	World Bank	https://data.worldbank.org/indicator/EN.POP.DNST	2021	30 Mar 2023

continued on next page

Table A1 *continued*

Principle	Subprinciple	Parameters	Subparameter	Final Score									Source	Link	Year	Access date
				INO	THA	SIN	VIE	MAL	PHI	CAM	BRU	LAO				
	Creativity and Innovation	Start-up environment	Quantity of start-ups	0	66	71	60	100	57	…	…	…	Startup Blink Global Startup Ecosystem Index 2022	https://lp.startupblink.com/report/#lp-pom-box-30	2022	NA
			Quality of start-ups	18	1	100	0	4	2	…	…	…				
			Business environment	52	9	100	28	50	0	…	…	…				
		Creative output	Intangible assets	66	78	75	100	84	65	19	1	0	WIPO Global Innovation Index 2022 Creative Output Pillar	https://www.wipo.int/edocs/pubdocs/en/wipo-pub-2000-2022-en-main-report-global-innovation-index-2022-15th-edition.pdf	2022	NA
			Creative goods and services	26	64	100	58	72	49	17	0	35				
			Online creativity	5	7	100	21	10	4	4	6	3				
		City environment	Creative cities	6	32	100	6	17	10	0	0	0	UNESCO	https://wikitravel.org/en/UNESCO_Creative_Cities	2022	4 Apr 2023
	Tourism Safety	Safety and security (from WEF TTDI)	Business cost of crime and violence	18	0	100	23	27	0	5	…	5	WEF TTDI	https://www.weforum.org/reports/travel-and-tourism-development-index-2021/explore-the-data/	2021	30 Mar 2023
			Reliability of police services	45	6	100	58	52	3	0	…	21				
			Safety walking alone at night	53	10	100	27	0	30	23	…	3				
			Homicide rate	92	62	100	77	69	0	69	…	0				
			Global terrorism index	35	19	100	93	70	0	100	…	93				
			Organized violence, deaths	100	90	100	100	100	0	100	…	100				
		Health and hygiene (from WEF TTDI)	Physician density	15	35	100	31	62	19	0	…	8				
			Use of basic sanitation	57	95	100	67	100	43	0	…	33				
			Use of basic drinking water	74	100	100	88	91	79	0	…	50				
			Hospital beds density	7	71	93	100	57	0	0	…	36				
			Accessibility of healthcare services	59	48	100	59	78	0	11	…	37				
			Communicable disease incidence	26	37	100	37	21	0	5	…	11				

continued on next page

Table A1 *continued*

Principle	Subprinciple	Parameters	Subparameter	Final Score									Source	Link	Year	Access date
				INO	THA	SIN	VIE	MAL	PHI	CAM	BRU	LAO				
Collaborative partnerships	Smart Governance	E-government online services	Institutional framework	100	87	100	75	100	75	50	38	0	United Nations E-Government Survey 2022 – Online Service Index	https://desapublications.un.org/sites/default/files/publications/2022-09/Web%20version%20E-Government%202022.pdf	2022	NA
			Content provision	100	60	60	80	100	40	60	40	0				
			Services provision	69	69	100	58	67	62	20	55	2				
			E-participation	63	73	100	38	59	32	3	30	0				
			Technology	50	60	90	50	100	40	50	40	11				
		Open government information	Open Data Inventory score	64	21	100	34	42	51	0	35	18	ODIN 2020/21 – Open Data Watch	https://odin.opendatawatch.com/data/Download	2022	29 Mar 2023
		Prioritization of travel and tourism industry (based on WEF TTDI)	Travel and tourism government expenditure	94	16	100	0	4	20	98	…	80	WEF TTDI	https://www.weforum.org/reports/travel-and-tourism-development-index-2021/explore-the-data/	2021	30 Mar 2023
			Comprehensiveness of travel and tourism data	100	79	25	0	25	57	18	…	32				
			Timeliness of travel and tourism data	100	100	100	100	100	100	100	…	0				
			Travel and tourism capital investment	21	0	100	47	37	13	53	…	50				
	Public–Private Collaboration	Public–Private Partnerships	Assessment of country's adherence to the best regulatory practices	68	36	73	63	32	100	16	…	13	World Bank	https://databank.worldbank.org/source/ppps-regulatory-quality#	2018	2 Apr 2023
			Investment value per PPP Project	100	8	15	23	7	36	0	…	73	World Bank	https://bpp.worldbank.org/economy/LAO	Total PPPs during 2014–2018	2 Apr 2023

… = data not available; ASEAN = Association of Southeast Asian Nations; B2C = business-to-consumer; BRU = Brunei Darussalam; CAM = Cambodia; CO_2 = carbon dioxide; ICAO = International Civil Aviation Organization; IMD = International Institute for Management Development; INO = Indonesia; ITU = International Telecommunication Union; LAO = Lao People's Democratic Republic; MAL = Malaysia; NA = not applicable; PHI = Philippines; PPP = public–private partnership; SIN = Singapore; THA = Thailand; TTDI = Tourism and Travel Development Index; UNCTAD = United Nations Conference on Trade and Development; UNESCO = United Nations Educational, Scientific and Cultural Organization; UNWTO = United Nations World Tourism Organization; VIE = Viet Nam; WEF = World Economic Forum; WIPO = World Intellectual Property Organization.

Note: In case of access data, "NA" represents that data is taken from a report and not from a database.

Source: Authors' analysis of data sources mentioned above.

Table A2: Technological Pillars of Tourism 4.0

Main Technological Pillars of Tourism 4.0 and Relevant Literature			
Pillar	Description of the Technology	Technology in Hospitality (Tourism Industry)	Authors
CPS	Cyber-physical systems (CPS) are defined as integrated and interconnected physical and virtual arrangements based on computation, communication, and control systems.	CPS consists of two aspects: (i) interconnection of the physical and cyber worlds, which enables access to the real-time data; and (ii) smart data management, analytics and computational capability.	Lee, Bagheri, and Kao (2015)
IOT	Internet of Things (IOT) involves interconnectivity among physical devices and cyber worlds.	IOT enables interactions with tourists and collection of real-time tourist data, thus creating personalized and localized services, and accurate evaluation of tourists' behaviors and preferences.	Munir, Kansakar, and Khan (2017); Kansakar et al. (2019)
AR	Augmented Reality (AR) involves the combination of real and virtual objects in a real environment, synchronization of real and virtual objects, and interaction in 3D and real time.	AR provides tourists with more personalized services and several additional benefits. It enables tourists to share and exchange information and opinions with other tourists in large networks.	Van Krevelen and Poelman (2010); Kounavis, Kasimati, and Zamani (2012)
VR	Virtual Reality (VR) simulates reality. VR is "a computer simulated (3D) environment that gives the user the experience of being present in that environment."	VR provides people with opportunities for virtual travel with a low cost and contributes to sustainable tourism.	Desai et al. (2014); Wiltshier and Clarke (2016)
Big data	Big data analytics are related to recent technological developments, which cope with the data processing and analysis.	In the hospitality sector, big data include internal and external big data. Data can be classified based on their characteristics and type, and hospitality ecosystem actors can access and use these data to prepare strategic business plans and manage their operations in a dynamic way.	Ben Youssef and Zeqiri (2020); Buhalis and Leung (2018)
AI and robots	Artificial Intelligence (AI) and robots are used in workplaces to maintain contact with people in a shared nonindustrial environment and can replace humans in research and development activities.	AI and robots are used in the hospitality sector to create more personalized and unique experiences, for instance at traveler information centers in the airport.	Tung and Law (2017); Horváth and Szabo (2019); Ben Youssef and Zeqiri (2020)

Source: Taken from Table 1 of A. Zeqiri, M. Dahmani, and A. B. Youssef. 2020. Digitalization of the Tourism Industry: What Are the Impacts of the New Wave of Technologies. *Balkan Economic Review*. 2. pp. 63–82.

REFERENCES

Abbas, J., R. Mubeen, P. T. Iorember, S. Raza, and G. Mamirkulova. 2021. Exploring the Impact of COVID-19 on Tourism: Transformational Potential and Implications for a Sustainable Recovery of the Travel and Leisure Industry. *Current Research in Behavioral Sciences.* 2 (10228). 100033.

Ajuntament de Barcelona (Barcelona City Council). n.d. Pilot Project: IOT & Big Data – Tourism Management. A presentation on IOT and Big Data in Action, Use Case: Sagrada Família. Barcelona. https://ajuntament.barcelona.cat/turisme/sites/default/files/documents/iot_bigdata_consell_turisme.pdf.

Alford, P. and R. Jones. 2020. The Lone Digital Tourism Entrepreneur: Knowledge Acquisition and Collaborative Transfer. *Tourism Management.* 81 (5). 104139.

Asian Development Bank (ADB). 2021. *Developing Agriculture and Tourism for Inclusive Growth in the Lao People's Democratic Republic.* Manila.

ADB. 2023. *Narrowing the Development Gap: Follow-Up Monitor of the ASEAN Framework for Equitable Economic Development.* Manila.

ADB and United Nations World Tourism Organization (UNWTO). 2021. *Big Data for Better Tourism Policy, Management, and Sustainable Recovery from COVID-19.* Manila: ADB.

Australia and New Zealand Banking Group Limited (ANZ). 2018. *The Digital Economy: Transforming Australian Businesses.* Melbourne.

Baggio, R. 2008. Symptoms of Complexity in a Tourism System. *Tourism Analysis.* 13 (1). pp. 1–20. https://doi.org/10.3727/108354208784548797.

Ben Youssef, A. and A. Zeqiri. 2020. Hospitality Industry 4.0. and Climate Change. *GREDEG Working Papers.* No. 2020-23. Université Côte d'Azur, France: Groupe de REcherche en Droit, Economie, Gestion (GREDEG CNRS).

Buhalis, D. and A. Amaranggana. 2013. Smart Tourism Destinations. In Z. Xiang and I. Tussyadiah, eds. *Information and Communication Technologies in Tourism 2014.* Cham: Springer. https://doi.org/10.1007/978-3-319-03973-2_40.

Buhalis, D. and R. Leung. 2018. Smart Hospitality—Interconnectivity and Interoperability Towards an Ecosystem. *International Journal of Hospitality Management.* 71 (1). pp. 41–50. https://doi.org/10.1016/j.ijhm.2017.11.011.

Li, C. 2017. A Preliminary Discussion on the Connotation of Digital Economy. E-Government. 9. pp. 84–92.

Consumers International. 2021. Consumers International Guidelines for Online Product Safety. London. https://www.consumersinternational.org/media/368991/online-product-safety-guidelines-report_final.pdf.

Chung, N., H. Lee, J. Ham, and C. Koo. 2021. Smart Tourism Cities' Competitiveness Index: A Conceptual Model. In W. Wörndl, C. Koo, and J. L. Stienmetz, eds. *Information and Communication Technologies in Tourism 2021.* Proceedings of the ENTER 2021 eTourism Conference. 19–22 January. pp. 433–438.

Darcy, S. and T. J. Dickson 2009. A Whole-of-Life Approach to Tourism: The Case for Accessible Tourism Experiences. *Journal of Hospitality and Tourism Management.* 16 (1). pp. 32–44. https://doi.org/10.1375/jhtm.16.1.32.

Dredge, D., G. T. L. Phi, R. Mahadevan, E. Meehan, and E. Popescu. 2019. *Digitalisation in Tourism: In-Depth Analysis of Challenges and Opportunities.* Brussels: Executive Agency for Small and Medium-Sized Enterprises, European Commission.

Economic Research Institute for ASEAN and East-Asia (ERIA). 2022. *Study to Develop A Framework on Sustainable Tourism Development in ASEAN in the Post COVID-19 Era.* Jakarta.

European Commission. 2022. Leading Examples of Smart Tourism Practices in Europe. https://smart-tourism-capital.ec.europa.eu/system/files/2022-05/Best%20Practice%20Report_2022_Update.pdf.

GIZ. 2020. *The Tourism Value Chain: Analysis and Practical Approaches for Development Cooperation Projects.* Bonn.

Go, F. M. and R. Govers. 2000. Integrated Quality Management for Tourist Destinations: A European Perspective on Achieving Competitiveness. *Tourism Management.* 21 (1). pp. 79–88.

Graci, S. 2020. Collaboration and Partnership Development for Sustainable Tourism. In J. Saarinen, ed. *Tourism and Sustainable Development Goals.* London: Routledge. https://doi.org/10.4324/9780429324253.

Gretzel, U. 2017. Smart Destination Research: State of the Art. Paper prepared for the Conference on Smart Tourism Destinations: New Horizons in Tourism Research and Management. Alicante, Spain. 25–27 October. http://dx.doi.org/10.13140/RG.2.2.22062.41289.

Gretzel, U., M. Singala, Z. Xiang, and C. Koo. 2015. Smart Tourism: Foundations and Developments. *Electron Mark.* 25 (3). pp. 179–188.

GSMA. 2016. *GSMA Smart Cities Guide: Crowd Management.* https://www.gsma.com/iot/wp-content/uploads/2016/10/GSMA-Crowd-management-case-study-web.pdf

Heeley, J. 2011. Public: Private Partnership and Best Practice in Urban Destination Marketing. *Tourism and Hospitality Research.* 11 (3). pp. 224–229.

Horváth, D. and R. Z. Szabó. 2019. Driving Forces and Barriers of Industry 4.0: Do Multinational and Small and Medium-Sized Companies Have Equal Opportunities? *Technological Forecasting and Social Change.* 146. pp. 119–132. https://doi.org/10.1016/j.techfore.2019.05.021.

Hudson, S. and L. Hudson. 2017. *Marketing for Tourism, Hospitality and Events: A Global and Digital Approach.* London: Sage Publications.

International Monetary Fund (IMF). 2018. Measuring the Digital Economy. Policy Paper. Washington, DC.

Institute of Southeast Asian Studies (ISEAS) – Yusof Ishak Institute. 2021. Assessing Digital Economy Policies in Six Southeast Asian. ISEAS Perspective. 50. https://www.iseas.edu.sg/wp-content/uploads/2021/03/ISEAS_Perspective_2021_50.pdf.

Jakulin, T. J. 2016. Systems Approach for Contemporary Complex Tourism Systems. *International Journal for Quality Research.* 10 (3). pp. 511–522.

Kansakar, P., Munir, A., and Shabani, N. (2019). Technology in the Hospitality Industry: Prospects and Challenges. *IEEE Consumer Electronics Magazine.* Vol. 8, Issue 3, May 2019.

Kim, Y. J., D. K. Lee, and C. K. Kim. 2020. Spatial Tradeoff Between Biodiversity and Nature-Based Tourism: Considering Mobile Phone-Driven Visitation Pattern. *Global Ecology and Conservation.* 21. e00899. https://doi.org/10.1016/j.gecco.2019.e00899.

Kounavis, C. D., A. E. Kasimati, and E. D. Zamani. 2012. Enhancing the Tourism Experience through Mobile Augmented Reality: Challenges and Prospects. *International Journal of Engineering Business Management.* 4 (1). https://doi.org/10.5772/51644.

Lee, J., B. Bagheri, and H. A. Kao. 2015. A Cyber-Physical Systems Architecture for Industry 4.0-Based Manufacturing Systems. *Manufacturing Letters.* 3. pp. 18–23. https://doi.org/10.1016/j.mfglet.2014.12.001.

McKinsey Global Institute. 2019. Digital Identification: *A Key to Inclusive Growth.* https://www.mckinsey.com/capabilities/mckinsey-digital/our-insights/digital-identification-a-key-to-inclusive-growth.

Mittal, A. 2022. *Catalog of Technical Standards for Digital Identification Systems.* Washington, DC: World Bank.

Munir, A., Kansakar, P., and Khan, S. U. (2017). IFCIoT: Integrated Fog Cloud IoT: A novel architectural paradigm for the future Internet of Things. *IEEE Consumer Electronics Magazine.* https://doi.org/10.1109/MCE.2017.2684981

Okeleke, K. and J. Joiner. 2022. *Digital Societies in Asia Pacific: Progressing towards Digital Nations.* GSM Association.

Organisation for Economic Co-operation and Development (OECD). 2016. *Consumer Protection in E-commerce: OECD Recommendation.* Paris: OECD Publishing. http://dx.doi.org/10.1787/9789264255258-en.

OECD. 2019. *An Introduction to Online Platforms and Their Role in the Digital Transformation.* Paris: OECD Publishing. https://doi.org/10.1787/53e5f593-en.

OECD. 2020a. *Building Back Better: A Sustainable, Resilient Recovery after COVID-19.* Paris.

OECD. 2020b. Preparing Tourism Businesses for the Digital Future. In *OECD Tourism Trends and Policies.* Paris: OECD Publishing.

OECD. 2020c. *Safe and Seamless Travel and Improved Traveller Experience.* OECD Report to G20 Tourism Working Group. https://www.oecd.org/cfe/tourism/Safe-and-seamless-travel-and-improved-traveller-experience-OECDReport-for-the-G20-TWG_merged.pdf.

OECD. 2021. *The Role of Online Marketplaces in Enhancing Consumer Protection.* Paris.

Pacific Economic Cooperation Council (PECC). 2021. *Primer on Economic Integration Issues Posed by the Digital Economy.* Singapore.

Pantano, E. and D. Stylidis. 2021. New Technology and Tourism Industry Innovation: Evidence from Audio-Visual Patented Technologies. *Journal of Hospitality and Tourism Technology.* 12 (4). pp. 658–671.

Pencarelli, T. 2020. The Digital Revolution in the Travel and Tourism Industry. *Information Technology and Tourism.* 22 (3). pp. 455–476.

Rachinger, M., R. Rauter, C. Müller, W. Vorraber, and E. Schirgi. 2019. Digitalization and Its Influence on Business Model Innovation. *Journal of Manufacturing Technology Management.* 30 (8). pp. 1143–1160. https://doi.org/10.1108/JMTM-01-2018-0020.

Desai, P. R., P. N. Desai, K. D. Ajmera, and K. Mehta. 2014. A Review Paper on Oculus Rift-A Virtual Reality Headset. *International Journal of Engineering Trends and Technology.* 13 (4). pp. 175–179. https://ijettjournal.org/archive/ijett-v13p237.

Silverio-Fernández, M., S. Renukappa, and S. Suresh. 2018. What Is a Smart Device? A Conceptualisation within the Paradigm of the Internet of Things. *Visualization in Engineering.* 6 (1). 3. http://dx.doi.org/10.1186/s40327-018-0063-8.

Tang, H. C. and A. Cortez. 2023. Paving an Even Path in Asia's Digital Economy: Role of Regional Cooperation in Inclusive Digital Transformation. East Asia Blog Series. 17 February. ADB-PRC Regional Knowledge Sharing Initiative.

TransUnion. 2022. *Global Digital Fraud Trends: Rising Customer Expectations amid Evolving Fraud Threats.* https://www.transunion.com/content/dam/transunion/global/business/documents/2022-fraud-trends-report.pdf.

Tung, V. W. S. and R. Law. 2017. The Potential for Tourism and Hospitality Experience Research in Human-Robot Interactions. *International Journal of Contemporary Hospitality Management.* 29 (10). https://doi.org/10.1108/IJCHM-09-2016-0520.

Turner, J. R. and R. M. Baker. 2019. Complexity Theory: An Overview with Potential Applications for the Social Sciences. *Systems.* 7 (1). 4. https://doi.org/10.3390/systems7010004.

Tussyadiah, I., S. Li, and G. Miller. 2019. Privacy Protection in Tourism: Where We Are and Where We Should Be Heading for. In J. Pesonen and J. Neidhardt, eds. *Information and Communication Technologies in Tourism 2019.* Cham: Springer. https://doi.org/10.1007/978-3-030-05940-8_22.

United Nations (UN). 1999. *UNCITRAL Model Law on Electronic Commerce with Guide to Enactment 1996.* Vienna. https://uncitral.un.org/sites/uncitral.un.org/files/media-documents/uncitral/en/19-04970_ebook.pdf.

United Nations Conference on Trade and Development (UNCTAD). 2021. *Digital Economy Report 2021—Cross-Border Data Flows and Development: For Whom the Data Flow.* NY: United Nations Publications.

United Nations Economic Commission for Europe, Inland Transport Committee. 2020. *Transport Trends and Economics 2018–2019: Mobility as a Service.* Geneva. https://unece.org/DAM/trans/main/wp5/publications/Mobility_as_a_Service_Transport_Trends_and_Economics_2018-2019.pdf

United Nations Office of the High Representative for the Least Developed Countries, Landlocked Developing Countries and Small Island Developing States (UNOHRLLS) and World Trade Organization (WTO). 2022. *Digital Trade: Opportunities and Challenges.* NY: UNOHRLLS / Geneva: WTO. https://www.un.org/ohrlls/sites/www.un.org.ohrlls/files/joint_study_on_digital_trade_2022_by_ohrlls_and_wto.pdf.

United Nations World Tourism Organization (UNWTO). 2020. *Priorities for Tourism Recovery.* Madrid. https://webunwto.s3.eu-west-1.amazonaws.com/s3fs-public/2020-05/UNWTO-Priorities-for-Global-Tourism-Recovery.pdf.

van Krevelen, D. W. F. and R. Poelman. 2010. A Survey of Augmented Reality Technologies, Applications and Limitations. *International Journal of Virtual Reality.* 9 (2). pp. 1–20. https://doi.org/10.20870/IJVR.2010.9.2.2767.

Wang, D. 2013. China's Smart Tourism Destination Initiative: A Taste of the Service Dominant Logic. *Journal of Destination Marketing and Management.* 2 (2). pp. 59–61.

Wiltshier, P. and A. Clarke. 2016. Virtual Cultural Tourism: Six Pillars of VCT Using Co-Creation, Value Exchange and Exchange Value. *Tourism and Hospitality Research.* 17 (4). pp. 1–12. https://doi.org/10.1177/1467358415627301.

World Economic Forum (WEF). 2014. *Smart Travel – Unlocking Economic Growth and Development through Travel Facilitation.* Geneva. https://www3.weforum.org/docs/GAC/2014/WEF_GAC_TravelTourism_SmartTravel_WhitePaper_2014.pdf.

WEF. 2018. *The Known Traveller: Unlocking the Potential of Digital Identity for Secure and Seamless Travel.* Geneva. https://www.accenture.com/_acnmedia/pdf-70/accenture-wef-the-known-traveller-digital-identity.pdf.

WEF. 2020. Advancing Digital Trade in Asia. Community Paper. Geneva.

World Travel and Tourism Council (WTTC). 2019. *Visa Facilitation: Enabling Travel and Job Creation through Secure and Seamless Cross-Border Travel.* London.

WTTC. 2020. Global Guidelines for Safe and Seamless Traveller Journey. London. https://wttc.org/Portals/0/Documents/Reports/2021/SSTJ-Biometrics%20and%20Digital%20Identity%20Global%20Guidelines.pdf?ver=2021-02-27-120737-970.

World Intellectual Property Organization (WIPO) and UNWTO. 2021. *Boosting Tourism Development through Intellectual Property.* Geneva: WIPO.

World Bank. 2019. *The Digital Economy in Southeast Asia: Strengthening the Foundations for Future Growth.* Washington, DC.

Yallop, A., et. al. 2021. The digital traveller: implications for data ethics and data governance in tourism and hospitality. *Journal of Consumer Marketing.* Vol. 40 No. 2, pp. 155-170. https://doi.org/10.1108/JCM-12-2020-4278.

Zeqiri, A., M. Dahmani, and A. B. Youssef. 2020. Digitalization of the Tourism Industry: What Are the Impacts of the New Wave of Technologies. *Balkan Economic Review.* 2. pp. 63–82.

Zhang, L. 2012. On the Basic Concept of Smarter Tourism and its Theoretical System. *Tourism Tribune.* 27 (5). pp. 66–73.

Zhao, X., X. Mei, and Z. Xiao. 2022. Impact of the Digital Economy in the High-Quality Development of Tourism—An Empirical Study of Xinjiang in China. *Sustainability.* 14 (20). 12972. https://doi.org/10.3390/su142012972.